Ancient Mythologies

Ancient Mythologies

Charles Kovacs

Wynstones Press

First published by Resource Books 1990
Reprinted by Wynstones Press 1999 and 2008

© Resource Books and Wynstones Press.
All rights reserved. No part of this publication may be reproduced by any means whatsoever without the prior written consent of the publisher.

The right of Charles Kovacs to be identified as the Author of this work has been asserted by him in accordance with the Copyright, Designs and Patents Act 1988.

Cover illustration:
Sidhartha by Daniel C Bryan
Acrylic and Japanese paper on canvas.

Published by Wynstones Press
Stourbridge
England.
www.wynstonespress.com

A catalogue record for this book is available from the British Library.

ISBN 978 0 946206 52 0

Printed and bound in the UK by
CPI Mackays, Chatham ME5 8TD

Contents

India

Manu and Atlantis	10
King Sangara's Horse	16
Baghira and the River Ganges	23
Indra, the Warrior God	27
The Fishermen's Catch	33
The Sons of Pandu	38
The Hermit and the Elephant	68
Rama and Hanuman	72
Buddha, the Enlightened One	86
Krishna, A God in Disguise	100
The Peasant's Reward	108
The Tiger and the Monkey	112

Persia

Ahura Mazda and Ahriman	116
Hushang Discovers Fire	119
King Djemshid's Golden Dagger	122
Zarathustra and the Kingdom of Light	125

Babylonia

The Land of Two Rivers	144
Marduk, the God Who Knew No Fear	148
Gilgamesh and Eabani	152

Egypt

The Gift of the Nile	166
Isis and Osiris	169
Appendix	189
Further Reading	190

Preface

Waldorf School teachers in the English-speaking world are at a disadvantage compared with their German colleagues. A teacher in Hamburg can be certain to find background material by anthroposophical authors in any subject. Few books of this kind are available in English and the material in public libraries is often at odds with the spirit of Waldorf education.

Charles Kovacs (born 1907 in Vienna), a class teacher at the Edinburgh Rudolf Steiner School, wrote his extensive Main Lesson notes day by day from class 1 to 8 to help colleagues in search of suitable source material. Subsequently, the texts have been used and appreciated by teachers in Edinburgh for many years.

Although presented verbatim in lesson format, it should be understood that the text represents the way in which a particular teacher taught a particular group of children. But the content of the stories, the mood the teacher tried to engender and the appropriate narrative style provides valuable information, particularly for a teacher presenting a subject for the first time. With new Waldorf Schools springing up continuously, and with few experienced teachers to staff them, there is a real need to make material of this kind available.

Finally, a word to those unfamiliar with Waldorf education. Springing out of the pedagogical impetus of the Austrian philosopher Rudolf Steiner (1861 – 1925), the Waldorf School curriculum aims to awaken much more than the mere intellect. Waldorf Schools all over the world seek to educate the whole being of the growing child, that each may develop their truly human and spiritual potential.

Myths of
India

Atlantis and Manu

This year you will hear some stories of people who lived a long, long way back in time at the very beginning of history. We will start with the people who lived in ancient India. Later on you will also hear about the people of ancient Persia, Babylonia and Egypt. They are all stories from countries far away and of times long ago, stories of mighty gods, noble heroes and great adventures.

Now the people who told some of these stories lived a long time ago; so very long ago that we would have to count back 10,000* years to reach the time they lived on earth. And at that time, 10,000 years ago, the world looked quite different. There were no towns or cities in Britain. There were no people at all because the whole of Europe lay under a thick cover of ice and snow. Today ice and snow many feet deep can be found all year round at the North and South Poles. But 10,000 years ago it was like that all over Britain, France, Germany and Norway. All the countries of Europe were covered in ice and snow, so nobody lived in that part of the world at all.

But there were parts of the world where it was warmer. Today, stretching between Europe and America there is an enormous wide ocean. Even the fastest ships need four or five days to cross this ocean, while the slower ones take about a week. And this vast ocean of rolling, tossing waves between Europe and America is called the Atlantic.

* See *Appendix page 189*

But 10,000 years ago there was an enormous island in the middle of the Atlantic. It was much bigger than the island of Britain and when an island is very, very large then it is no longer called an island; it is called a continent. Australia, for instance, is such a big island that it is a continent. Where there is now only the endless water of the ocean, there was once a great continent and it was known as Atlantis. But it is no longer there. Atlantis has disappeared and you will hear how this happened.

In Atlantis there was no ice and snow. It was much warmer. Plants grew and both people and animals could live there. But I don't think you would have liked it very much if you had to live in Atlantis, for the whole continent was covered all year round by mist and fog. There was always swirling mist so the people of Atlantis could never see a blue sky or a bright sun. And they would certainly never see a rainbow, for a rainbow is only visible when at least part of the sky is clear. Of course, the people who lived in Atlantis did not mind the fog and mist. They were used to it, just as people born in Africa are used to great heat.

Now you have heard that the whole world was different; ice and snow covered Europe while the great continent of Atlantis was shrouded in mist. But the people who lived in Atlantis were also different from us in many ways. They had powers which we no longer have; they had powers which we would call magic. They had, for instance, the power to make plants grow more quickly or more slowly.

Just think how convenient it would be for a farmer today if he could make his crops grow faster, or stop the wheat from ripening when it rains hard for many days. Nowadays, the farmer has to wait for nature; he can't speed up or slow down the growth of his crops. But 10,000 years ago, people had powers which have since disappeared, just as the whole continent of Atlantis has disappeared.

The people who lived in Atlantis could also use their power to make animals grow bigger, or smaller. They had no cats or dogs as we have now, but if they wanted their pet cow to be the size of our dogs they could make it stay small. But if they wanted a cow as big as an elephant they could make it grow that large.

Of course these wonderful powers could also be misused. They could be used against other people in a very cruel way. Now in Atlantis it was usual for a king or a rich man to own many slaves. In those days people kept slaves, and such slaves could never leave their master. A slave belonged to the master like an ox or a cow belongs to a farmer. And if it suited a king or a rich man he could, by using these magic powers, stop people from growing to their normal size. Such a man could, for instance, make slave children stay little so that they were like dwarves. Or if a king wanted big men for his soldiers and bodyguards, he made children grow to twice the ordinary size. They were made to grow into giants. So you see, the use of these powers brought much suffering, for it is very wicked to change the normal size and shape of the human body.

But there also lived in Atlantis a good and wise man whose name was Manu. Manu never used his magic powers to change other people's natural shape. It made him very sad to see how the misuse of magic caused great unhappiness when people were prevented from growing to their natural size and shape.

When Manu felt sad he would often go to the banks of a little stream. One day as he sat by the stream, looking down into the water, he saw a tiny little fish darting hither and thither, trying to escape from a large fish. Manu did not like to see any creature suffer and he bent down, wondering what he could do to help. Then a strange thing happened; that little fish spoke. It called to him: "Help me, protect me and I will reward you! Take me out of the water, put me in a water-jug at your home, and you will never regret it!"

The big fish was just opening its mouth to swallow the little fish when Manu scooped the little one out. He hurried home and put it in a jug with fresh water. He looked after it and fed it and the fish grew very quickly. Soon the jug was too small and Manu put it into a large water tank. But it kept on growing, and when the tank was too small the fish spoke again and said: "Take me to the great river!"

Manu carried the fish, which was now quite heavy, to the river. Then the fish spoke again and said: "Come back soon, for I will grow larger still and need your help." When Manu came back a few days later that marvellous talking fish had grown even larger. And the fish said to him: "If I stay here I will soon be so large that I will fill the river, and it will overflow its banks. I want you to take me to the ocean." By now it was quite a burden to carry that heavy fish. Yet Manu knew that this was no ordinary fish but a messenger from God, and so he did as he was told.

When he had put the fish into the ocean, it spoke once more and said: "Now the time of your reward has come. Know then, wise Manu, that this great island of Atlantis is doomed. Very soon rain will fall as it has never rained before. For weeks and months and months it will rain, and rain, and rain. The water in the rivers and the water of this ocean will rise, and the whole of Atlantis will sink. And that will be the end of the magic power which the people of Atlantis have so misused. But you, wise Manu, must start to build a great wooden ark or ship. And on this ship you must take with you only people who have not misused their powers, or those who have no magic powers at all. You must also take seeds from every plant with you. And when the wooden ark is ready I will come again to help."

Manu obeyed and began to build the big wooden ark. He also found men and women who had not used magic for wicked things, or people who had no such powers. And he had barely finished when the rain began to fall and the waters began to rise.

But where did all the water that fell as rain come from? You remember I told you of the ice and snow that covered Europe. Now at that time, the sun began to shine with more heat than ever before. The ice and snow began to melt, and a lot of water flowed into the ocean. That water went up like steam and became clouds, and from the clouds came the rain.

It poured down steadily and the water in the ocean rose steadily. Manu, and the people he had collected together, hurried on to their wooden ark. Then the fish appeared yet again, but by now it had grown as big as a whale (which is as big as a house). The fish said: "Take a big rope. Fasten one end of the rope to the ark and the other end to my tail, and I will take you and your comrades to a new land. There you can make a new start without magic powers which have only brought misery to people."

So it was done. Manu and his people sailed away, pulled by the big fish, while endless rain poured down. And, just as the fish had said, the ocean waters rose higher and higher until the whole of Atlantis was covered by the sea.

Ever since, Atlantis has remained deep down under the ocean. And to this day, the ocean where Atlantis used to be is called the Atlantic Ocean. But the heat of the sun which caused the great flood had also melted all the ice and snow which had covered Europe. So it became a land where plants could grow and people could live. But for a long time it remained without people and was covered in dense forests.

The great fish took the ark, with Manu and his people aboard, to a far away land called India. It was a long journey of many months. They sailed away in the heavy rain which drowned Atlantis but, as they travelled on, the rain ceased and they saw for the first time a blue sky. Manu and his companions had only known the mist and fog of Atlantis, but the rain had washed all the mist away. When it stopped they saw a clear sky for the first time, and arching right across the blue was a wonderful rainbow. So with a great rainbow overhead, the first they had ever seen, Manu and his comrades arrived in India.

King Sangara's Horse

You have heard the story of the wise Manu and his people; their escape from the terrible doom that came upon Atlantis, and how the great fish brought them to a new land called India. In India, Manu and his companions had to make a new beginning. They could no longer use magic powers to make things grow faster and slower. Instead they had to work hard, then plant the seeds and wait for the sun and for the rain. Things would only grow and ripen for them in the right season. In India, however, the weather and the seasons are quite different. They do not have spring, summer, autumn and winter; the four seasons as we know them. In India there are only three seasons; the hot season, the wet season and the cool season.

During the hot season the sun shines with a very fierce heat. For months and months there is not a cloud in the sky. The grey earth is baked hard and plants shrivel and die. At noon the heat is so great that neither men nor animals move about. They lie and rest wherever they can find a little shade. It is so hot that if you put a raw egg on a stone in the sun, it is hard-boiled in a quarter of an hour.

After three or four months of heat, the first clouds appear. Soon the whole sky is covered with dark clouds. There are flashes of lightning, mighty peals of thunder roll, and then the rain comes down. But this is not rain as we know it. It pours down in sheets of water and you can only see for a few yards.

It pours and pours for several hours every day and, as the water comes down, the plants begin to grow. After a few days, the earth is covered with a green carpet; there is new life everywhere.

A few months later the wet season comes to an end. The rain stops and the skies clear. Now comes the most pleasant of the seasons, the cool season. The cool season of India is like a warm summer in Europe, but it is still nice and cool compared with the burning hot season. Then, three months or so later, the days begin to get warmer and warmer. And so the hot season comes again.

Now Manu and his companions had to watch these seasons very carefully. It would not have been wise to plant the seeds of their crops in the hot season, for they would die under the fierce heat of the sun. They had to plant their seeds just at the beginning of the wet season because it is the rain that brings new life to the plants.

Manu also taught his companions to look up to the heavens and to worship the gods who bring the seasons. He told them: "Just as there is a season of rainfall which gives life to all things so, in the heavens, the highest god created the world and gave life to it. And this highest god is called Brahma. But as the plants grow and ripen in the cool season after the rain, so there is another god who takes care of the world which Brahma has created. This second god who protects life is called Vishnu. And the third god, who is like the burning heat of the hot season when the plants wither and die, is called Shiva."

You see, just as the people who had come to India had three seasons, so they also looked up to three gods: Brahma, the highest, who created all things; Vishnu, who takes care of all things and protects them, and Shiva, who destroys all that must wither and die to make room for new life.

In those days people not only worshipped and prayed

to the gods, they also made sacrifices. When a peasant had harvested his crop, for instance, he took some flour and made some cakes. He took them to a stone altar on which a fire was burning, and put the cakes into the flames. While they burnt away, he prayed to the gods for their blessing and a good harvest the next year. And the more a man sacrificed in the flames on the altar, the more blessings and good fortune the gods would send him.

The people in India who looked up to Brahma, Vishnu and Shiva, and made sacrifices to them, were very fond of telling stories of great marvels, very fanciful stories. One of these strange and fanciful tales was about a king who wanted to sacrifice a white horse to the gods.

The king's name was Sangara. He was a mighty and powerful king who had many wives and, from these wives, so many children that one could hardly count them. He had a whole army of sons so many were they. The king wanted to make a great sacrifice to the gods, a very special sacrifice so, in return, the gods would have to grant him every wish. He had many beautiful horses, and he decided that the most beautiful of them, a snow white stallion, would be killed and burned on the altar.

But the gods Brahma, Vishnu and Shiva did not want to grant King Sangara every wish, nor did they want the white stallion to be sacrificed. So, the night before the sacrifice was to take place, the god Vishnu came down to earth and took on a human shape. He stole the white stallion, took it far away and hid it where no-one could find it.

The next morning there was great excitement when the white horse could not be found. King Sangara was furious, and he called together all his many sons and said: "Go and search everywhere for my white horse!" The princes went far and wide looking for the horse but they could not find it. But when they came back and told their father that they had searched in vain, he commanded: "Then dig deep into the earth. Perhaps the thief has hidden the horse in a cave deep down."

And all the many sons took spades and started to dig holes, many holes. They dug deeper and deeper into the earth, so deep that it hurt and the earth cried out in pain to Brahma. Then Brahma spoke to Vishnu and said: "You are the protector! Go down and protect the earth against the sons of King Sangara."

The great god Vishnu descended to earth again. Below him, he could hear the earth crying with pain from the big, gaping holes which the many sons of King Sangara had dug in their search for the horse. Vishnu, who did not want to frighten the princes with his true god-like majesty, appeared to them as a man. He called out to them: "Do not disturb Mother Earth with your useless digging. The horse is not down in the depths. I am the one who knows where King Sangara's white horse is."

When the many sons of Sangara heard him say he knew where the horse was hidden, they shouted: "Here is the thief who has stolen the horse!" And they all rushed at him and struck him with their spades. But Vishnu was a god not a man; when the spades touched him, a searing red hot flame leapt out. In one moment the princes, all of them, were burnt to ashes.

But their fate was even worse than being reduced to ashes. When people died of old age, or illness or in battle their souls left their bodies and rose up to heaven. But the sons of Sangara had, without knowing it, attacked a god. Although they had not known they were doing anything wrong, because they had turned against a god, their souls could not ascend to heaven and had to stay with the ash of their bodies.

Even Vishnu himself felt pity for them, but not even he, the god, could do anything. There was only one thing that would help carry the princes' souls to heaven, and you shall hear later what this thing was.

When the sad news of the death of the princes was brought to King Sangara, he cried bitter tears. He called his grandson and told him to go and collect the ashes. The grandson set out. After a long search he came to the place where the flame of Vishnu had burned the princes, and their ashes covered the ground.

On a rock nearby perched a great eagle, as if standing guard over all that remained of the sons of Sangara. When the grandson came near, the eagle spoke to him and said: "From Brahma, the Lord and Creator, I have a message for King Sangara. Great sadness has come to him, for not only have his sons been slain by the fire of Vishnu, but their souls are imprisoned in the ash of their bodies and cannot rise up to heaven. Yet, from this sadness great joy can come. For it is the will of Vishnu that these souls shall, in time to come, rise to heaven and be companions and friends of Vishnu himself."

"But how can this come about?" asked the grandson. "It can come about in this way," answered the eagle. "Far in the north of India there are the highest mightiest mountains in the world. They are called the Himalayas, which means the 'home of snow'. The tops of these mountains reach up into the clouds, eternal snow and ice cover the peaks and slopes. Those who have had the good fortune to behold the pure white beauty of the Himalayas say that nothing in the world can be compared to their shining majesty.

The eagle continued: "From the pure snow of the Himalayas there came forth a river called the Ganges. Its waters rushed down the slopes, leaping and dancing in waterfalls over cliffs and rocks until, down in the valley, they gathered in one mighty river that flowed through forests, glades and meadows to the ocean. Pure and clear were the waters of the Ganges, as pure as the snow from which they came. But so beautiful was the river that the gods wanted it for themselves. They took it away from earth and carried it up to the heavenly city, where only gods and the souls of good people can enjoy its beauty.

"If the river Ganges, the daughter of the Himalayas, can be brought back to earth, and if the ashes of the princes are then thrown into the river, the pure waters will wash away all the sins, all the mistakes, the princes ever made. Their souls will then rise up to Vishnu who will receive them with joy. Take, therefore, the ashes back to King Sangara. Tell him that from you, his grandson, there will come children, and from them other children. One of them will be so great and so good that he will be able to bring the river Ganges, the daughter of the Himalaya mountains, back to earth. He will then set free the souls of the princes imprisoned in their ashes."

So spoke the eagle, then it spread its powerful wings and rose into the air. The bird flew higher and higher, until King Sangara's grandson could no longer see it. And, as he had been told, the grandson collected the ashes and put them in a golden casket he had carried with him. When he had done this, he saw nearby the white stallion grazing peacefully. The boy took the golden box and the horse back to King Sangara.

When King Sangara heard that, one day, all his sons

would be companions of Vishnu, he was no longer sad. He prayed humbly that it would not be too long until he and his sons met in the heavenly city where Brahma and Vishnu and Shiva hold sway.

When King Sangara died his grandson became king. He was followed by his son. So the time came near when the river Ganges could, as the eagle had foretold, be brought back to earth.

Baghira and the River Ganges

From the story of King Sangara who wanted to sacrifice his horse, you also learnt something about the land of India itself. You remember it is a very hot country where there is never any winter. But you also heard that there are mountains called the Himalayas which are covered all year round with ice and snow. This is possible because of the enormous height of the Himalayas which are the highest mountains in the world. And at such terrific height snow and ice never melt.

Just imagine how curious this is: down below, at the foot of the mountains there can be the fierce, sweltering heat of the hot season. But up in the heights it is everlasting winter. It is a wonderful sight for travellers to look up from the burning heat of the Indian plains and see, in the far distance, an enormous range of snow-covered, white mountain-peaks.

From this pure white snow came the waters of the beautiful river Ganges, that great river which the gods loved so much that they took it away from the earth up to their heavenly city. But only the waters of the river Ganges could set the souls of the sons of King Sangara free from the ash of their bodies.

Now, as you heard, King Sangara died and his grandson became king. When he passed away, his son followed. And every king that came to rule gave much thought to the ashes which rested in the golden casket. Each king wondered what he could do to bring the river Ganges back to earth, and so help the poor souls of the princes.

After many, many years and many, many kings, there came a king whose name was Baghira. He was a man who cared very little for all the pomp and splendour in which kings lived at that time. Baghira did not care for his treasures of gold and jewels, or for the hundreds of servants ready to obey every command. Nor did he care for the great palace and the splendid gardens full of flowers and sweet fruit. What he did care for were the poor souls of the princes still bound to the ash in the golden casket.

Baghira spent many hours every day in deep prayer asking the gods to show him a way to help the princes and set their souls free. One day when he was praying the god Shiva appeared before him. The king fell to the ground and covered his face with his hands because the rays of light that came from the god hurt his eyes. Then Shiva spoke to him and said: "Fear not, King Baghira, I have come to you to tell you how the souls of the sons of Sangara can be set free, and how the beautiful Ganges river can be brought back to earth.

"We gods have powers far beyond anything a human being could ever have. We have power over life and death; the oceans obey us and the storms follow our command. Yet the gods, too, are bound by rules. But if a man gives up all the pleasures he could have in life; if a man denies himself everything he likes out of his own free will; if a man lives without a house, without money, without amusements, without comfort, without family or servants and if he then spends all his time in prayer; then for such a man even we, the powerful gods, must do whatever he wants of us."

And then Shiva said: "If you, King Baghira, are willing to take up such a life without pleasure or possessions, not for a week or months but for many years, then you can ask the gods to bring the river Ganges back to earth, and not even Brahma can refuse your wish."

Then Shiva disappeared and King Baghira set about becoming the kind of man the god had described. He told his ministers to rule the kingdom and he left the palace and the pleasures of the court to live by himself deep in a forest. His dress was only a piece of rough cloth, he slept under trees on the bare ground and ate nothing but some roots and berries he found in the forest. Baghira had no roof when the rains poured down and no shelter against the burning sun. His hair and beard grew long and he hardly ever saw any other human being.

The forests of India are full of wild animals. Herds of elephants crash their way through the trees, tigers pounce on their prey, poisonous snakes slither on the ground and giant snakes, which can strangle an ox, lurk in the trees. But the king had no weapons with which to defend himself. Yet in all the many years that he lived in the forest, alone and unarmed, he never felt any fear and none of the wild animals attacked him. And every day Baghira spent many hours in prayer.

The peasants who lived in a village near the forest would often speak of the holy man or hermit as they called him. Sometimes they would leave a bowl of milk where they knew he would find it. He would not have accepted any other food. And so the years passed until, one day, as the hermit was praying again, Brahma appeared before him. But now Baghira did not cover his eyes, for the years of harsh life and prayer had given him the strength to look at the gods. And Brahma said: "Tell me, what is your dearest wish and I shall give it to you." The hermit answered: "My dearest wish is that the river Ganges is brought back to earth to flow again from the Himalaya mountains through the land of India."

Brahma, who would like to have kept the beautiful river, the daughter of the Himalayas, in his heavenly city, could not refuse the hermit Baghira's wish. But there was one difficulty. If that mighty river had fallen straight down from heaven, it might have shattered mountains and knocked a deep hole in the earth. So the god Shiva, with his great strength, had to catch the river just before it touched the ground. He put it down gently on its course, from the Himalayas through India to the sea. There it still flows to this day and is called a holy river.

And the hermit Baghira went to the palace where he had once lived and took the golden casket. He threw the ashes of the sons of Sangara into the Ganges, and their souls flew upwards and joined the god Vishnu. Then as the hermit bathed in the river, his soul left his body and rose to Brahma.

Indra, the Warrior God

The Warrior God and the Giants
There are many rivers flowing down from the Himalayas into India. India actually takes its name from the Indus, which is one of those rivers. But of them all, the Ganges is the holy river and it is still regarded that way today. And because all Indians know the story of how the ash of the sons of Sangara was thrown into the Ganges and their souls rose to heaven, they burn their dead and still throw the ashes into the Ganges. So you see, although the story is many thousands of years old it is still important for the Indian people today.

You also remember King Baghira who became a hermit and gave up all possessions and all comforts. To this day you can see many hermits like him in India, both men and women who live as Baghira had lived. Sometimes these hermits have quite strange powers and one day you will hear a story of the powers which some of these people have.

You also heard about the three great gods, Brahma, Vishnu and Shiva. But these were not the only gods which the people of India worshipped, and still worship today. There are many other gods, and one of them is Indra, the son of Brahma.

Now when the rains came, when thunder rolled and lightning flashed, the people of India said: "The god Indra, the son of Brahma, drives his golden chariot which is pulled by two fiery horses called Bold and Brown. In his left hand Indra holds the reins, but in his right he holds a magic stone called the thunder stone. When he throws the thunder stone, lightning rips the sky and peals of thunder shake the world. But every time he hurls this magic stone it comes back again into his hand."

Indra, lord of the thunderstone and the golden chariot, was also the God of War, the god to whom warriors prayed when they went into battle. He was the god of all soldiers and all warriors because he, himself, was waging war against evil giants who were the enemies of both gods and men.

One of these evil giants, called Sambara, lived on the summit of a high mountain. There, up in the heights, he had his stronghold and he used to stand, leaning on his weapon, which was an enormous staff as long and broad as ten tree trunks together. His hair stuck out from his head like pieces of wire, and his beard reached down to his waist.

When Sambara looked down from his mountain top and saw a little peasant village in the valley below, an evil grin would appear on his face. He would look for a large, heavy boulder, a great piece of rock, and roll it to a place on the mountain-top directly above the little village. Then he would give the rock a push with his big staff. At first it would roll slowly, but then it would hurtle faster and faster, taking more and more smaller stones and rocks along with it. In the end a vast mass of pebble, sand and dust would rush down the slope with terrible speed and crash on the village. It would smash and shatter the little huts. The whole village would be buried under the rocks and sand, and most of the people would die under the crushing weight that had fallen on them.

From his mountain top, Sambara would look down on the destruction. He would roar with laughter and jump into the air with glee so that the whole mountain shook. But the poor peasants, who lived near the foot of the mountain, could not move away because that was where they had their little plots of land. They lived in fear and worry for no-one knew which village the giant would pick next for his wicked jokes. So the peasants made sacrifices to the great warrior god, Indra, who fights the giants, and prayed to him for help and protection against Sambara.

One day, at long last, Indra listened to their prayers. He mounted his golden chariot, took his thunderstone with him, and drove his fiery steeds at a gallop across the sky to the mountain stronghold of the giant.

Sambara had just made another rock ready to bring death and destruction to an innocent village. When he saw Indra coming in his golden chariot, he was wild with rage that his favourite game should be interrupted. He roared and bellowed with fury, and took his big staff and hurled it at Indra. But the god threw his thunderstone at the great staff that flew through the air. There was a flash of lightning, and the staff was shattered into a thousand little pieces.

When Sambara saw his weapon was smashed he howled with anger, and he broke off the whole peak of the mountain and sent it flying against Indra. But the god already had the thunderstone in his hand again. He threw it and, this time, the magic stone drove the great mountain peak back. It sailed through the air and struck the giant on the head. He fell down with a crash and was dead.

The peasants down in the valley could not see what was going on for the mountain top was hidden in mist and clouds. But they heard a terrific noise and thunder, which made the mountain shake and tremble. Then everything became very quiet. Never again did rocks fall from above, so they knew that Indra had come to their rescue.

When all the other giants came to know what had happened they swore they would revenge Sambara. They decided that Indra, as well as human beings, would suffer for the death of a giant who had only amused himself. And tomorrow you will hear what they did.

Indra Slays the Dragon

You have heard how the other giants had sworn to revenge themselves on Indra and on human beings for the death of Sambara. Now the king and leader of the giants was a very ugly dragon, with the very ugly name Vritra. His body, which was as big as a mountain, was covered with red scales, horns grew from his head, and his eyes were like red-hot coals. One day the dragon said to the giants: "There is one thing that will hurt Indra and human beings at the same time." – "What is it?" shouted the giants. "It is quite simple," said Vritra. "We shall steal Indra's cows."

Now what are Indra's cows? They are the clouds. The clouds, which come at the end of the hot season and bring the life-giving rain, are the 'cows' of Indra. Just as we human beings are nourished by the milk from cows, so the plants are nourished by the rain from the clouds. And just as herds of cattle graze in the fields, so the clouds, the herds of Indra, move across the sky.

So the dragon Vritra and his giants went out and stole all Indra's cows. They drove them away and kept them hidden. Then the hot season came in India. It came, but it did not go. After three months, four months, ten months, a year, the rainy season had not yet come. It was still dry and hot. A second year passed, then a third and a fourth. Ten years later still not a drop of rain had fallen. And even after twenty years there were no clouds in sight.

Under that endless dry, burning heat, all the crops had long since withered and shrivelled. No new seeds could be planted, and the earth was baked so hard that a spade could not have cut into it. Even in the dense forests, the trees first lost their leaves, then died and stood bare and black. The smaller rivers had all dried up and even the Ganges, which drew its water from the snows of the Himalayas, had become a tiny stream; a trickle of water so muddy that not even animals could drink from it.

The people of India – men, women and children – died in their millions. Those who survived, the people who lived near the Himalaya snows, were so weak that they could not burn the dead. Never before had there been so much misery and suffering among human beings. And so passed thirty nine years!

Of course, the people prayed to all the gods. They prayed especially to Indra, but even the gods, even Indra, dared not go to war against the terrible Vritra. Then, in the fortieth year, when it seemed that before long even the last people would die out, Indra roused himself to save the people of India before it was too late.

Armed with his thunder-stone, he climbed into his chariot and drove Bold and Brown towards the mountains where Vritra and his giants had their stronghold. When Vritra saw Indra coming he roared so terribly that both earth and heaven shook and trembled. The dragon spread his horny wings, and rose up into the air to meet the god and destroy him. Indra flung his thunder-stone at the dragon, but it fell on the monster's hard red scales and could do no harm.

When the giants saw this they laughed and cheered, for they thought this would be the end of Indra. But the thunder-stone returned to his hand and, as the dragon reared up, he threw it again. This time the god aimed at the under side of Vritra which was not covered with scales. There was a thunderclap, a flash of lightning as bright as the sun, and Vritra fell down from the sky like a stone and was dead. The other giants fled in terror when they saw their king vanquished.

Then Indra saw a cave in the mountainside, but a great rock barred the entrance. The god hurled his thunder-stone, and the rock shattered into tiny pieces. Hidden inside were Indra's cows and, after forty years, out they poured. Soon, all over India, the sky filled with clouds. Then the rain arrived and it poured and poured. From the mountains and hills torrents of water rushed down, filling the river beds and bringing new life to plants.

Even today the people of India remember Indra's great deed of slaying Vritra. When the hot season comes to an end, when peals of thunder and flashes of lightning announce the coming of the life-giving rains, the Indians make cakes and burn them on altars to show their gratitude to Indra. The arrival of the rainy season in India also marks the beginning of autumn. And just as we celebrate the festival of St Michael, the fighter against the dragon, in autumn, so the people of India celebrate Indra's victory over the dragon Vritra.

The Fishermen's Catch

You have heard how the people of ancient India looked at the clouds and said: "Floating up the in the sky are the 'cows' of Indra. The rain which comes from the clouds nourishes all plants, just as we are nourished by the milk from our cows." For these people, the cows here on earth and the clouds in the sky were so much alike that, in their language, they had only one word for clouds and for cows. In this ancient language the word *go* meant a cow but also a cloud. If a man said "My *go* has a calf," then you knew he meant a real cow. However if he said: "There is a dark *go* in the sky," then you knew he was talking about a cloud.

Cows and oxen were the most important animals in the world to the people in ancient India. They pulled the ploughs over the fields so that seeds could be planted, and they gave milk from which butter and cheese could be made. Even the cow dung was very useful. You see, in such a hot country you don't need a fire to keep warm, but you do need fire for cooking. But the forests of trees which could be used for firewood were often far away and, in those days, there were no railways or lorries to carry wood over long distances. So how did a poor peasant find fuel for his fire? He took a shovel and a basket, collected the dung, and left it in the sun to dry. Dry dung burns quite well and the peasants of India still use it today, as they have done for thousands of years.

But there is one very important thing: the people of India never ever ate the meat of cows or oxen. They were so grateful for all the things the cow gave them, that they thought it would be quite wrong to kill it and eat it. And it is still so today: no-one in India would slaughter a cow, an ox or a calf and eat the meat. And there is a story that will show you how highly the cow is regarded.

In India there were many priests of the Brahma. (A priest is something like the minister in a church.) The building in which they worship their gods is called a temple, and the priests who hold their service in such temples are called Brahmins. The Brahmins of India were greatly respected by the people, not only because they held the services, but because they knew the laws and they could tell people what was right or wrong. They also knew when it was the best time to sow the seeds of various crops; in those days there were no books or calendars to show you what week or month it was. Only the Brahmins knew the right time. And they also knew of many herbs to cure people when they fell ill. So you see, a Brahmin was a very important person.

Now one Brahmin who had served the gods and helped the people for many years decided that he would leave the temple and live alone in the forest to give all his time to prayer. And so he lived without a roof over his head, and for food he had only the berries he found in the forest.

This Brahmin loved all living creatures, but most of all he liked to go to a nearby river to watch the fish playing in the water. His hard life and devoted prayers had given him powers which ordinary people do not have. One of the powers was this: he could go down under the water, lie on the bottom of the river and stay there as long as he liked. Since he was so fond of fish, he used to lie under the water often and the fish got so used to him that they played around him and swam through his long hair without any fear.

One day some fishermen came to this part of the river. They sailed down the river in a boat and threw a big net, a very strong net, out into the water. When they pulled it in, there were not only plenty of fish in the net but also that holy man, the Brahmin.

The fishermen were very surprised that they had caught a living man with their fish. When they recognised him as the holy man, the Brahmin of the forest, they were terribly afraid that he would be cross and destroy them with his great powers. They quickly took him out of the net, and told him how sorry they were. But the Brahmin said: "I am not cross with you. You are fishermen. You must make a living and you did not know you would catch me in your net. But now, as you have caught me, I am going to stay with the fish. When you sell the fish you have to sell me as well!"

"That's impossible," cried the fishermen. "The great king of this country himself told us to bring him fish from this river. How can we go and tell him he should pay us for the fish, and also for you?" But the Brahmin said: "Take me and the fish to the king and then we shall see what happens." So the fishermen did as they had been told. They took the holy man and the fish to the king. They explained how they had caught the Brahmin with the fish in their net, and that they had to sell both fish and man.

The king was terrified. He was afraid of offending the holy man who, with a curse, could destroy him. So there stood the king in his splendid royal robes, in fear and trembling before the hermit, whose rags and unkempt hair and beard still dripped with water. Then the king said: "Please tell me what I shall pay these fishermen. I will give them anything you want." And the Brahmin answered: "First pay them for the fish."

Now, in those times, so long ago, people did not have money. Coins and paper money did not exist. If you wanted to buy something, you could only do it by swapping one thing for another which is called bartering. Ordinary people would swap or barter some eggs, perhaps, for a pound of butter or maybe a calf for a piece of cloth. But a king, who had gold and jewels in his treasure-house, would pay with some of his treasure for anything he wanted to buy.

So the king said: "I will give these men a golden cup for their fish." – "Yes," said the hermit, "that's quite a good price. But what are you going to pay them for me?"

Again the king was worried that he might offend the holy man. So he said: "For you I will give them half of all my treasures." – "What," shouted the Brahmin. "Do you think I am only worth that rubbish of dead metal and stones?" – "No, no," cried the king, "they can have all my treasure." But the Brahmin only shook his head. "Half my kingdom," cried the king. Again the Brahmin shook his head. "My whole kingdom," said the king in despair. "Not even a hundred kingdoms like yours are worth as much as I am," answered the Brahmin.

By now the king was desperate. He did not know what to do, and he asked the hermit to wait a day so that he could think about the right price to pay for a holy man. Deep in thought, the king went off by himself for a walk into the forest. Suddenly, coming towards him, he saw another hermit. He hurried to him, bowed deeply, and told him his worries. Then the other hermit said: "The life of any human being is priceless. All the treasures and all the kingdoms in the world cannot pay for a human being. But men cannot live without cows, just as the plants cannot live without the rain that comes from

Indra's cows in the sky. And, in this way, a cow is worth as much as a man."

The king thanked the other hermit and hurried back to the palace. He found the Brahmin the fishermen had caught and said: "I will give them a cow for you." The hermit smiled. "This is the right price," he said, and he blessed the king and returned to his forest.

The Sons of Pandu

King Pandu's Misfortune
From the stories we have learnt several things about life in ancient India. You heard that people in those days had no money. If they wanted to buy something they had to barter, to exchange something else for it.

We also learnt that cows were, and still are, treated as sacred animals which must not be killed. And, in the last story, we discovered that the priests or Brahmins were held in such great honour that a king was willing to give his whole kingdom to pay for a holy man. But how did it come about that the Brahmins were so greatly respected and honoured?

When Manu brought his companions to India he divided them into three groups. He said to the first group: "You are the clever, the wise ones. You will be like the head of Brahma, you will be the priests and teachers." To the second group he said: "You are not so clever but you are strong and brave. You will be warriors and kings. You will be like the arms of Brahma." And to the third group he said: "You are not so clever with your heads, you are not so strong and brave as the others, but you are willing, faithful workers. You will be peasants and tradesmen such as carpenters, tailors and merchants. You will be like the legs of Brahma."

This division still exists in India today. The son of a Brahmin can only marry a girl who is another Brahmin's daughter, and the son of a peasant, even if he becomes very rich, could not marry the daughter of a warrior or a Brahmin.

THE SONS OF PANDU

So far, the stories you have heard have been about the gods or about Brahmins and holy men. But today we begin a story about warriors, about great heroes.

There once lived a king whose name was Pandu. But great misfortune came to him. One day, while out hunting with bow and arrow, King Pandu accidentally shot and killed a holy man. He was so sorry about what he had done – although he had not done it intentionally – that he no longer cared to be king. He decided to live in the forest as a hermit, and so pay for the death of the holy man.

King Pandu had five sons but they were all still too young to become king in his place. So Pandu went to his brother and said: "Brother, my heart is heavy because I cannot forget the holy man I have killed. I do not wish to be king any longer, I want to become a hermit myself. Will you rule the kingdom and look after my sons until one of them is old enough to become king?" And the brother answered: "I will certainly do what you want. Your sons shall be brought up with my own sons and I shall look after them well."

So King Pandu went into the forest, accompanied by his queen who would not leave him. Pandu's brother, whose name was Dritarushtra, became king. But this brother was blind. The blind king did as he had promised and the five sons of Pandu were brought up together with his own two sons.

One day the princes were playing in the garden with a ball. They threw it between them and enjoyed the game until one of them missed his aim, and the ball fell into a deep well. They all rushed to the well and looked down; there was the ball, floating on the water, but so far down that no-one could reach it. They took two long sticks and tried to get hold of it but the ball fell back into the water each time. The young princes were losing hope that they would ever play with that ball again when they saw an old Brahmin watching them with a smile.

They had never seen him before but they rushed eagerly to him and asked him to help get their ball back. The Brahmin said: "What? You are royal princes and you can't even get a ball out of a well? Look, it is quite easy." He plucked a blade of grass from the ground. He took it between his fingers, threw it down the well and it stuck in the ball just like a dart. That surprised the princes but it did not bring the ball back.

"The ball, the ball. Get the ball back again," they shouted. "Patience, patience," said the Brahmin, "I have only just started." Then he took another blade and threw it down and it got stuck in the first blade of grass. Then he threw a third blade which stuck in the second one, and he carried on until the blades of grass were like a rope which came up to the top of the well. Then he pulled and brought the ball up.

The princes thanked him but then they cried: "Teach us your skill, teach us to aim as well as you!" – "Then go to Dritarushtra, the blind king, and tell him that Drona has come," said the Brahmin. The Brahmin Drona was famous for his wisdom and skill, and the blind king was well pleased that the princes had found such a good teacher. Drona instructed the seven princes; the five sons of Pandu and the two sons of the blind king. He taught them all the things princes had to know; from the verses of wisdom which had come down from Manu, to how to use sword and bow and arrow with skill.

Now, one of the sons of Pandu, Arjuna, was keener than all the others in the use of bow and arrow. One evening when he was eating, the lamp went out but he continued with his meal. And Arjuna thought that since he could carry food to his mouth even in the dark he could, with practice, hit a target in the dark. From that time onwards, he practised with bow and arrow in both daylight and darkness.

And when Drona heard the twang of Arjuna's bowstring in the night air, he came to him and praised him.

The Deed of Arjuna
You have heard that the seven princes were instructed by the wise Brahmin in the skilled use of arms, and that they also had to learn many verses. You see, in those days there were no books because the art of reading or writing had not yet been invented.

Stories like the ones you have been hearing and many, many more were told by one person to another. Older people told stories to the young, so that when the young people grew old they could pass them on to the next generation. The Brahmins, too, told stories to the people; to the warriors and peasants, and the stories they told were quite specially long and important. And if a boy was to become a Brahmin it was part of his training that he learnt these stories, these long stories, by heart.

But there was one thing which made it a bit easier to learn such long stories. They were all poems, very long poems that were all in verse. And although there weren't any books, people had something much better; they had wonderful memories. They had much better memories than we have today so they could learn long, long poems by heart much better than we can.

For instance, a Brahmin of those ancient days learnt about 10,000 lines by heart, and once he knew them he never forgot. And because these long poems were faithfully learnt, they were passed on exactly, word for word, from older Brahmins to younger Brahmins for thousands of years, and not a single word was forgotten or changed.

Just think of it; one generation of Brahmins came, learnt the poems, passed them on to the next generation and died. Countless Brahmins have come and gone but the poems have lived on, unchanged. In our time, now that we have reading and writing and books, the poems are, of course, all written down and printed. But even today the Brahmins learn a great part of them by heart, although much less than in the old days. And the story of the five sons of Pandu and the two sons of the blind king Dritarushtra is one of those the Brahmins have been telling to the people of India for many thousands of years.

The wise Brahmin Drona had become the teacher of the seven princes. They learnt from him the wisdom and knowledge which future kings would need in those times; how to rule with justice and fairness and how to lead an army into battle. He taught them good manners; he taught them to ride horses and to drive chariots, and he taught them the skilled use of sword, battle-axe, bow and arrow.

But the sons of Pandu were quite different in their skills. The oldest, Yudishtira, was also the wisest of the brothers. He was very clever and when the teacher asked a difficult question, it was always Yudishtira who could answer it first. But Yudishtira was not quite as good with weapons as his brothers. The second prince, Bishma, was not so clever. He was usually the last to find the answer to a question, but he was terribly strong. His favourite weapon was the mace; a strong rod or stick with a round piece of metal on the top. When Bishma hit with his mace, stones were shattered to dust, and iron broke as if it were thin wood.

Then came two princes who were twins, Natiala and Sahadeva. They were not as clever as Yudishtira, nor as strong as Bishma, but no one could handle horses better than the twins. When they rode their horses they could make them gallop much faster than the others. And the last one was Arjuna. As you have already heard, he was good with all weapons. No one had such a sure aim with bow and arrow, or could drive a chariot as well as he did.

These were the five sons of Pandu. The two sons of the blind king also became strong, brave warriors but they were often jealous of the other princes, their cousins, and their accomplishments.

One day Drona, the teacher, wanted to test his royal pupils. He asked the blind king for some gold and jewels and out of them he made a little bird with eyes of red rubies. The Brahmin put the bird high on the branch of a tree. Then he called the princes and said: "I will now call each of you in turn. When your turn comes take aim at the eye of the bird with your bow and arrow, but do not shoot until I tell you." He turned to the oldest of the princes, Yudishtira, and said: "It's your turn first."

Yudishtira took his bow and arrow and aimed carefully, ready to let fly at Drona's command. But Drona said: "Before you shoot, tell me, can you see the bird?" – "Yes," said the prince, "I can see the bird." And Drona said: "Can you see the tree?" – "Yes," said Yudishtira. "Can you see me and the other princes?" – "Yes, I can see you all," was the answer. Drona asked the same questions three times, and every time he got the same answer: "I can see the bird, the tree, and all of you."

When he had asked for the third time, Drona sighed and with a sad voice he said: "Put the bow and arrow down, Yudishtira. It is not for you to shoot this arrow." Then Drona called the other princes, one after the other. They took aim, and three times he asked them the same questions he had asked Yudishtira. When they gave the same answer, he told them to put the bow and arrow down and would not let them shoot at the bird.

At last it was Arjuna's turn. Again Drona asked: "Do you see the bird, the tree, the other princes and me?" But Arjuna answered: "No, my master, I do not see anything but the bird." – "Describe the bird to me. What does it look like?" cried Drona. "I cannot tell you, answered Arjuna, "for I see only the red rubies of his eyes." When Drona heard this answer he was delighted and he cried out: "Shoot." Arjuna's arrow went soaring up and hit the bird. It fell down from the tree, and everyone could see the arrow had pierced the head through the ruby red eyes.

You see, when you have a task to do you must forget everything else and pay attention only to the task. Arjuna was the only one who had understood this and so he could pass the test. But his brothers and cousins could not.

The Journey to Benares
You have heard about the long poems all in verse that the Brahmins of India learned by heart and told the people. The story of the sons of Pandu is the most famous of them.

There is no one in India today, even the poorest peasant living in a little hut, who has not heard about the deeds of Arjuna or does not know who Yudishtira was. Just as you all know about David and Goliath, or the story of Joseph and Mary and the child in the manger because they are stories found in the Bible, so the story of the sons of Pandu comes from a kind of holy book which everybody knows in India.

You have heard how the two sons of the blind king, Dritarushtra, grew up together with the five sons of Pandu. But as time went on, the sons of the blind king became more and more jealous of their five cousins.

The elder of the blind king's two sons was called Durodhana. As they all grew up there was one thought Durodhana could not bear, one thought that filled his heart with hatred, envy and wild fury. It was the thought that one day when his father died, Yudishtra, the eldest son of Pandu, would become king. Little by little, Durodhana began to think to himself: "I should be king when my father dies and not any one of the sons of Pandu."

One day Durodhana went to his father and said: "Surely, it is not right that Yudishtira should rule the kingdom. I am your son, and I should become king after you." Although the blind king would really have wanted the throne for his own son, he cried out: "It cannot be! I have promised my brother Pandu that his eldest son shall rule when I die." But Durodhana answered: "What does it matter that you made a promise to Pandu. As you know, his wife, the mother of the five, who stayed with Pandu in the forest has come back with the news that Pandu has died. She is staying with her sons, and now Pandu is dead there is no-one who can stand up against you. Surely you, as the king, have the power to deal with the sons of Pandu."

Then Durodhana said: "If you dare not do anything against them openly, there are ways to get rid of them by cunning. Listen to me, I have a plan for killing all five of them and their mother, yet nobody will be able to blame you or me." When the blind king heard his son's plan, he forgot the promise he had given his dead brother and agreed with Durodhana to bring about the death of the five brothers by a wicked, murderous plan. You will soon see what they had in mind.

On the banks of the holy river Ganges there was, and still is today, a famous city called Benares. One day when the king and all the princes and courtiers were together, Durodhana began to praise the beauty of that city. He spoke of the splendid buildings, the great parks and gardens and the wide sweep of the river Ganges. When the five sons of Pandu heard about this beautiful city, they said: "We would like to see Benares and its fine buildings. And we would love to see the holy river Ganges, the daughter of the Himalayas."

Immediately the blind king said: "Then you shall go there my dear nephews. And you, and your dear mother, shall all travel as befits royalty. You shall each ride to Benares on your own elephant." Then Durodhana said: "Splendid are the buildings of the famous city but none of them is worthy enough for you, my dear cousins. I will send my own master-builder to Benares. He is a craftsman beyond praise, and he will build a house for you that will make all the other buildings look like beggar's huts. You, and your dear mother, shall have a truly royal house, a house fit for kings."

Of course, the five brothers were most grateful for such kindness and they looked forward to their stay. While they and their mother prepared everything for the journey, Durodhana sent his master-builder to Benares so that the house would be ready when they arrived.

But Durodhana spoke to the master-builder in secret

and said: "It is my desire that the five sons of Pandu shall never return from Benares. Therefore do not build them a house out of bricks or stones. Build a wooden house that will catch fire easily and quickly and, one night, when they and their mother are asleep, set fire to it. When this Pandu-brood has been destroyed, I will reward you with as much gold as an elephant can carry." And the master-builder promised he would do what Durodhana wanted.

Now you all know what carpenters do to give a wooden table or cupboard a glossy shine. They put a varnish or polish on it. In the far-away countries of the east; in India, but also China and Japan, they have a specially smooth and shiny varnish. Because it is made from the resin of pine trees, it has a very pleasant smell but it is also highly inflammable; that is it catches fire and burns very easily.

So the master-builder hastened to Benares. He got workmen together and they started to build a very beautiful house out of pine, which burns more quickly than any other wood. When it was finished the master-builder painted the inside and outside of the house with a thick layer of varnish. It was a beautiful sight when the sun shone on the smooth polish of the house and made it gleam. There was no house like it in the whole of Benares.

Next door, the master-builder put up a little house for himself so that he could creep out easily at night and would not have far to go to set fire to the great wooden house. He thought that as soon as the fire was burning, he would flee in haste and claim his reward from Durodhana.

The shining, polished house was ready and the five brothers and their mother arrived. The elephants on which they had travelled were put in stables in another part of the city. So the royal princes and their mother went to see the beautiful house which their cousin Durodhana had asked his clever master-builder to make for them

Escape from the Flames

The five sons of Pandu and their mother arrived in Benares and entered the beautiful wooden house with the shiny varnish that the master-builder had made for them.

Now you remember that the wisest of the brothers was Yudishtira. While the others were admiring the house and saying how generous cousin Durodhana had been, Yudishtira went from room to room. He sniffed the sweet scent of the varnish, and he looked at the walls of pine boards from which the house had been built.

When he had looked at everything, Yudishtira came to his brothers and his mother and said: "You have little reason to be so pleased with this house, for it needs only a small spark to turn the whole building into blazing fireworks. Do you think it is just for fun that this house has been built from materials which will burn like the stacks of wood on which people burn their dead? No, I tell you the whole house is a trap in which our cousin Durodhana hopes to catch us, and burn us to death."

The other brothers would not believe him at first but the more they thought about it, the more they came to see that Yudishtira was right. Then the wise Yudishtira said: "Listen to me, I will tell you how we can spoil Durodhana's wicked plan. Let us dig a deep hole in the ground here inside the house. From the hole we will dig a long underground passage that will come out far away at the edge of the forest. And through this tunnel we will all escape." Bishma, the strong brother, cried: "Yes, we shall make a passage, but when it is ready we will not wait for our enemy to set fire to the house. We, ourselves, shall start the fire and escape, then Durodhana will think we have all perished in the blaze."

During the night, when no one could watch them, the brothers set to work to dig the hole and the long underground passage. In the morning the work was finished, and the hole covered with wooden planks so that no-one could see what they had done. Of course, the evil master-builder knew nothing of this. He was waiting for a very dark, moonless night when he could creep into the house without being seen, and start a fire.

But the brothers did not wait. One night, when the master-builder was soundly asleep, Bishma set fire to the big house. While the flames were spreading, the brothers and their mother lifted the wooden planks, climbed down into the hole and made their way through the underground passage and out into the forest. Meanwhile the master-builder's hut caught fire and he was burnt to death. When morning came the big house and the little house, with the master-builder in it, were nothing but a heap of ashes. And everybody thought that the five brothers and their mother had also perished in the blaze.

When the news that the princes were dead reached Durodhana and his blind father, they pretended they were very sorry. Durodhana was in tears over the loss of his dear cousins and the blind king did not eat for a whole day to show he was so sad that he'd lost his appetite. But very soon after, the blind king announced that, since his dear nephews had all died, his own son Durodhana would become ruler and king after him.

In the meantime the brothers and their mother had fled from the forest to a far-away city. Here the five sons of

Pandu disguised themselves as Brahmins, so that no-one should know they were still alive. Now it happened that the king of this city had a very beautiful daughter whose name was Draupadi. Many princes wanted to marry her, but it was difficult to decide who was most worthy to become her husband.

One day the king called the best bow-makers of his court and, on his orders, they made a great strong bow, so stiff that it was nearly impossible to bend it. Then the king announced that a great contest would be held. The first man who could shoot an arrow from the bow through a ring hanging on a thread from a tree would win the hand of the princess.

When the day of the contest came, kings and princes arrived from all over India, and each one hoped to marry the beautiful Princess Draupadi. But at such a great festival there were not only hopeful kings and princes but also many Brahmins and huge crowds of onlookers. Many thousands of people came and they all waited for the king and his daughter to arrive so that the contest could begin. And among the crowd, disguised as Brahmins, were the five sons of Pandu.

Arjuna wins the Hand of a Princess
The contest for the fair Princess Draupadi was a great festival. Around the edge of a green field, galleries had been built which were filled with throngs of nobles, courtiers, ladies, and all the kings and princes who had come to try their strength with the great bow.

Down below, on the ground around the field, there were vast crowds of people from the city and the surrounding countryside, all eager to watch the contest.

There was also a special place where the Brahmins stood in their white robes, and among them were the five sons of Pandu. So great was the number of people who had come to see the contest that the roar of their talking was like the sound of great waves in the sea.

But all these many thousands of people fell silent when Princess Draupadi arrived with her father, the king. Sweet and gentle was her face, her eyes were big and dark and she smiled at the crowds. She wore a deep red silk sari. In her hand the princess carried a garland; a wreath with leaves of gold and flowers made of jewels which would be given to the winner of the contest.

When the king and the princess were seated, a Brahmin, whose hair and beard were white with age, approached an altar that stood in the field. On the altar was dry grass, and oil was poured over it. The Brahmin spoke the holy verses of prayer, kindled the fire and, as the flames rose, asked the gods to bless the contest.

Now the contest could begin and the first of the many kings who had come to gain the fair Draupadi came forward. He was a tall, fierce-looking man with a long black beard. He went down into the field, lifted the heavy bow which was taller than a man, put an arrow to the string and pulled. But although he pulled with all his strength, the bow would not bend, even slightly.

There was a tittering of laughter among the crowd; seeing a tall strong man pulling with all his might, without any result, seemed rather funny. That made the black-bearded king very angry. Red in the face and sweating with his efforts, he pulled again, but the bow did not bend. Shame-faced, the proud king had to put the bow down and make room for the next man. One after another, all the kings and princes who tried their strength failed. Some tried so hard that they strained their arms and could not use them for weeks after. No one could bend the bow.

Although Arjuna had come with his brothers only to watch the contest, when he saw the beautiful Princess Draupadi he felt he could never love any other woman but her. As one king after another put the bow down and left the field in shame, Arjuna came forward and stepped into the field. A buzz of excitement went through the crowd, for they saw a man dressed in the white robes of a Brahmin. Was a Brahmin to put the kings to shame? When Princess Draupadi looked at Arjuna, her heart seemed to take a little leap and she whispered a prayer to the gods to let him win the contest. But her father, the king, was ill-pleased when he saw a Brahmin take up the bow. He wanted a great prince or king as his son-in-law, not a priest who would never lead an army or fight a battle.

All eyes watched eagerly as the young man in Brahmin dress lifted his hands up in prayer to the gods. He took up the bow, put an arrow on the string, took aim and pulled. The bow bent as easily as if it had been the stalk of a flower. Then he let the arow fly. The arrow hissed through the air and straight through the ring hanging from the tree.

The crowd cheered and clapped; it was like thunder. Only the defeated kings and princes looked gloomy and angry, but the heart of Princess Draupadi was filled with joy. She stepped down from the seat, advanced towards Arjuna and placed the golden garland over his shoulders. Arjuna took her by the hand and led her to his brothers. Quickly they made their way through the crowds to the little house where their mother was waiting for them.

The old king, Princess Draupadi's father, was

completely taken by surprise. His daughter had been led away by this strange young Brahmin. Both had disappeared in the throng of people and he did not even know where they had gone. So the king called his son, Draupadi's brother, and said: "Go into the city. Find out where they have gone and then report to me what you have seen."

The brother went to the city and asked people if they had seen a Brahmin with a golden garland and a lady in a dark red sari. After a good deal of asking, he came to a little house with very thin walls. When he put his ear to the wall he could hear the people inside talking and, as he listened, he heard the names by which they called each other; Yudishtira, Bishma, Arjuna. Then, of course, he knew that these were not Brahmins but the famous sons of King Pandu.

Draupadi's brother hurried back. His father was overjoyed with the news that his beautiful daughter was not going to marry a Brahmin but a famous prince. He sent chariots and servants to the house to bring them all back to the palace. At first the brothers still tried to pretend they were only poor Brahmins but, in the end, they admitted to the king who they were. There was great rejoicing and a wedding feast was held.

Of course, the news that Princess Draupadi had married Arjuna soon spread. So the evil Durodhana and his father, the blind king, came to know that the five brothers were not only alive but had, through marriage, become relatives of a great and powerful king. Durodhana and his father did not like this news at all and they wondered what to do. In the end the blind king said: "I have already declared before the people that you should be my successor on the throne. But, if we try to be friendly with the five brothers, I am sure they will agree to take only half of my kingdom and you can keep the other half."

So a message was sent to the brothers. It said how pleased their uncle and cousins were to hear they had not perished in the fire, and invited them to come back so that the country could be fairly divided.

The five sons of Pandu were generous and forgiving. They went back to their own country with their mother and Princess Draupadi. And when the blind king begged them to take half the kingdom and leave the other half to cousin Durodhana, they willingly agreed so as to keep peace in the family. However, peace was not to last very long.

A Fateful Game of Dice

The blind king had persuaded the five brothers to share the great kingdom with his son Durodhana. The brothers were to take one half and Durodhana the other. But when the blind king divided the land, he did not divide it fairly. Durodhana received the half of the country where splendid cities stood, where great herds of cattle grazed on green fields and the peasants harvested rich crops every year. But the half given to the five brothers was either dense forest or stony ground. There were only small villages and the people were poor.

The five sons of Pandu where not disheartened, nor did they argue with Durodhana or his father. Instead they went and spoke to the poor peasants and said: "If we all truly work hard then this land, poor as it looks, will bear riches and wealth beyond anything Durodhana now has. The work of willing human hands can create wealth from barren deserts and wild forest."

So they all set to work. They cut down forests to make

room for fields and they built canals to bring the river waters to barren ground so that crops could be grown. They built splendid cities and drove out and killed robbers who had made the land unsafe for honest people. So great was the fame of the five brothers that people from all over India came to live in their country. In a few years the country that Yudishtira and his brothers ruled began to be prosperous. It had more people, more wealth, and more beautiful cities than the land of Durodhana. Durodhana's heart was eaten by envy and greed. He was no longer satisfied with his own share, he wanted the brothers' land as well.

In those days a warrior, a prince or a king could never refuse a challenge to a fight. If another king or warrior said: "Fight with me or you are a miserable coward," you would, of course, go and fight even if your enemy was stronger. There was, however, another kind of challenge which no warrior, prince or king could refuse: and that was a challenge to a gambling match. But they did not have playing-cards as we have now for gambling. People threw dice and if you scored more points with your throw than the other man you won. If you had fewer points you lost.

So it happened that the cunning Durodhana invited Yudishtira to a gambling match. He knew that the wise Yudishtira lost all his cleverness when he gambled. What was worse, once Yudishtira started to gamble, the excitement got such a hold on him that he could not stop, no matter how much he had already lost. And, being a warrior and a prince, he could not refuse his cousin Durodhana's invitation.

So the five brothers and the beautiful Queen Draupadi went to the city where Durodhana ruled, to take part in a gambling match which none of them would ever forget. They had brought gold and jewels with them and when Yudishtira and Durodhana began to roll the dice, they played, at first, for the treasure. Durodhana also had his treasure ready in case he should lose. But he had no fear of losing; his own dice were made so cunningly that they would always come up with the highest number.

As Yudishtira lost throw after throw, soon all the treasure he had brought along was Durodhana's. But by now the game had such a hold on him he could not stop. He said to Durodhana: "Now I will stake all my elephants against you. If I win, you give me back my treasure. If I lose, all my elephants are yours." But again Yudishtira lost. Then he lost all his horses, and then his cities, his fields and his cattle. In no time at all the whole country was lost.

But this was not the end. Yudishtira turned to his brothers and said: "I have nothing left to gamble with except you, my brothers. If I lose, I, myself, and you, my brothers, shall be slaves of Durodhana. But if I win, all I have lost shall be mine again." The brothers would not have let Yudishtira down and they agreed, as did Durodhana with a grim smile.

There were many onlookers at the game but they all were dead silent while this fateful throw was made. Yet when Yudishtira and Durodhana had each thrown their dice, it was clear that Yudishtira had lost. In despair he cried: "My brothers and I are your slaves, but Queen Draupadi is still free. For the last throw, Queen Draupadi against all I have lost." Again Durodhana nodded and the dice rolled. Again Yudishtira lost, and now Draupadi was lost as well.

Durodhana laughed aloud and cried: "Down on your knees before your master, you slaves! And you, slave woman

Draupadi, lie down under my feet as my foot stool!" But that moment there was a terrible noise. It was the croaking of hundreds of ravens that suddenly flew over the palace. And, as if in answer to the caw, caw of the ravens, there came a loud braying of all the donkeys kept in the king's stables. Then the old blind king came stumbling into the room where they were playing and shouted: "Don't you know that when ravens caw and donkeys answer it means the gods have sent a curse against you? What have you done, Durodhana, to bring a curse upon us?"

Durodhana told him that he had won the five brothers, Draupadi, and their whole country in a dice game. But the blind king shouted: "No, all you have gained is worth nothing if the gods curse you! Throw the dice again! If Yudishtira wins, all he has lost shall be his own again. But if he loses then he, his brothers and Draupadi shall be free. But they must give a promise to go and live for thirteen years in the forest as hermits. If they come out before that time they shall be slaves to you for breaking the promise."

Durodhana was not pleased with what his father told him. But because he was afraid of the curse of the gods if he kept the brothers as slaves, he agreed. Once again the dice were thrown, and again Yudishtira lost.

So the brothers and Draupadi changed their royal robes for the rough animal skins of hermits. They left their country, which would now become the possession of Durodhana, and went into the forest. Never once did any of them reproach Yudishtira; what had happened had happened and it was much more important that they helped each other in the hard years ahead. And it was while they were living in the forest that Arjuna was to find the weapon that, one day, would defeat the evil Durodhana.

The Bow called Gandiva

It was a harsh and grim life in the forest for the brothers and Draupadi. The queen had been used to the comforts of a royal court all her life but now they had no roof over their heads. They had to eat wild fruit, berries and roots, and they had nothing but fallen leaves for their beds.

Yudishtira, meanwhile, thought of the time when the thirteen years would be over. Durodhana would try to destroy them again and it seemed certain the five brothers would have to fight their cousin. But how could they fight against the great power he had gained by taking their country away from them?

One day, while Yudishtira was pondering this question, a Brahmin suddenly stood before him. The Brahmin said: "Your heart, O noble king, is troubled because of the great power and strength of your enemy. But no-one in the world could stand up against your brother Arjuna. If he goes into the mountains, up to the ice and snow of the Himalayas, and lives there by himself in deep prayer, a great god will appear to him. From that god he will receive the power to overcome your enemy."

Then the Brahmin went away and no-one knew where he had come from, how he knew Yudishtira's worries or where he had gone. But when Arjuna heard what the Brahmin had said, he set out immediately for the great mountains. Up there, where the snowfields looked down on him, there was even less to live on than there had been in the forest. A few withered leaves and the roots of some plants were all he could find.

Now if you live an ordinary life, as we all do, it would not be possible to live on so little. But Arjuna was not working, nor was he playing and enjoying himself. He sat in deep prayer most hours of the day and for many hours at night. If you live like that, the body draws its strength from prayer, not from food, and it requires only very little food to keep alive and healthy.

But there were also wild animals in the mountains and Arjuna had brought his bow and arrow to protect himself. One day he was disturbed in his prayers by a wild boar, a big wild pig with long sharp tusks. As the beast rushed toward him, he quickly took his bow and arrow and shot. The arrow hit the boar and it fell down. But how surprised was Arjuna when he noticed two arrows in the dead boar. Then he saw another hunter, tall and stately, who said: "This boar is mine. My arrow struck it. Or will you fight me for it?"

Arjuna was still a warrior so he could not refuse a challenge. He lifted his bow again and shot an arrow at the stranger, but the arrow simply disappeared in the other man, without doing him any harm. And so did a second and third arrow. Suddenly it came to Arjuna that his waiting was over and that he was now standing before the god he had come to meet in the mountains.

He sank to his knees. Before his eyes the stranger seemed to grow; his head appeared to touch the stars and even the Himalaya mountains looked tiny beside him. Arjuna also saw there was a great company with that stranger which seemed like hundreds of people; men, women, children, kings, priests and beggars. Then the stranger asked him: "Do you know any of these people you see now?" Arjuna answered: "My Lord, I do not know any of them, yet, somehow, they do not seem quite unknown either. They might be people I have known a long, long time ago." And the stranger said: "I am the god Indra, and I will reveal to you who these people are.

"You, Arjuna, and every other human being, are not here on earth for the first time. Long before you were born as Arjuna, you lived as a Brahmin. That Brahmin died, but his soul lived on and was born again as Arjuna. Yet before you lived as a Brahmin, you had another life on earth when you were a humble peasant. And even before that you had other lives.

"You have gone through many lives here on earth, Arjuna, and in those many lives you often helped other people. Do you see this woman? There was once great hunger and starvation in the land, and she was nearly dying. You were only a peasant then, and you had very little yourself. But what you had you shared with her, and so you saved her life.

"Do you see that boy over there? He was attacked by a tiger in the forest. You were a king and, although you had only a sword, when you saw it happen you came to the boy's rescue. You fought the tiger with your sword, drove it away, and saved the boy's life. All the people you see in this great company, Arjuna, are people to whom you have done some good. Each one has been grateful to you and thought of you with love."

Then the god Indra said: "Have you ever seen many little streams come together to become a great river? Even so have the thanks and the love of each of these people come together to become a great magic power. This power now rests in a magic bow and some arrows which I shall give you. No enemy can stand against you when you use this weapon, the bow called Gandiva. But remember one thing: the bow called Gandiva must never be used against enemies weaker than yourself. It must never be used for a wrong, unjust cause. It must only be used when all other weapons have failed."

Indra gave Arjuna a mighty, shining bow. The next moment the god and all the people had disappeared and Arjuna stood alone on the mountainside with the magic weapon, the bow Gandiva, in his hand. And the time was near when he would need it against the might of his wicked cousin Durodhana.

The Great Battle
When the thirteen years were over, the five brothers and Queen Draupadi left the forest. They had not forgotten all the things which Durodhana had done to them; the burning of the house at Benares or that they been given only half of the kingdom although, by right, it all belonged to them. Then Durodhana had even robbed them of that in a game of dice, and they had been forced to live in the forest for thirteen years. But now the time had come when they wanted to have what was, by right and in truth, their possession. So they sent a message asking Durodhana to give them back their half of the kingdom.

But Durodhana had, in those thirteen years, become mighty and powerful. He had not only great generals and thousands of brave warriors, but other kings had become his friends and allies and had promised to fight on his side if ever he were attacked. Even Drona, the teacher of the princes, had sworn to help him. And so Durodhana, proud of his own great power and of the many kings who would stand by him if there should be a war, gave the answer: "If the sons of Pandu were really warriors they would come and fight for what they want, and not ask for it like lowborn beggars."

Then the brothers knew that they would never get their land back, the land which had once belonged to their father Pandu, without a battle. But the five brothers also had friends. There was Draupadi's father, a great and mighty king, and there was also another king, Krishna, who wanted to help. People told strange stories about Krishna; that he was not a human being, but one of the gods who had been born as a man to help human beings in their fight against evil.

The whole of India was divided between those who took the side of Durodhana, and those who stood by the sons of Pandu. All over the country young men slung their bows over their shoulders, girded their swords round their waists, and left their homes to fight for Durodhana or Yudishtira.

Merchants buried their wealth under the earth for fear soldiers would steal it, and peasants quickly gathered their harvest before the armies trampled their fields. The terrible word war sounded from the snow-capped Himalayas to the cities on the sea-shore of India. And both mighty armies, the army of Durodhana and his friends and the army of Yudishtira and his friends, met on a great plain, called Kurukshetra.

The night before the battle, when thousands of brave warriors slept their last night on earth (for they would lose their lives in the coming battle) Krishna suddenly stood before Durodhana and said: "There can still be peace, and many lives saved, if you give to Yudishtira what belongs to him by rights." But Durodhana would not listen and Krishna left him.

Then in the early dawn, when all were still asleep, Krishna came to Arjuna and said: "Your cousin Durodhana wants battle and bloodshed rather than peace and agreement. But I will help you. I will drive your chariot into battle so that you have your arms free to slay your enemies." Yet Arjuna's heart was sad at the thought of having to fight his own cousin, and that so many brave men would lose their lives. But Krishna said: "Do not be too sad about those who shall die. For the soul never dies; it rises up from the body when that body dies. As men put away an old dress for a new one, so the soul puts away the old body and gains another."

So Arjuna was able to go into battle with a good heart. As the sun rose higher the trumpets sounded, and the many thousands of warriors took up their arms. The princes mounted their chariots and, with wild shouts, the two great armies rushed against each other. Terrible was the slaughter. The blood ran in red rivers over the stony ground of the plain of Kurukshetra, and dead bodies covered the earth like leaves in autumn.

Drona, who had once been the teacher of the princes, was now fighting against the brothers. His arrows never missed their mark and killed warrior after warrior. It was one of Drona's arrows which hit the father of Draupadi in the heart, and he fell, dead, from his chariot.

But Drona had a son who was also fighting against the brothers. And this son came up against the mighty Bishma, who was wielding his favourite weapon, the mace. Under the terrible blows of Bishma's mace, the son of Drona fell, dead. A great shout went up: "The son of Drona has fallen." When Drona heard this shout he lost heart, put down his bow and stepped from his chariot. In that moment a sword struck him and killed him. And the man who had struck Drona and killed him was Draupadi's brother, who had so avenged his father.

For eighteen days the battle raged. Sometimes it

seemed that Yudishtira's armies would win, and at others that the armies of Durodhana were closer to victory. But on the last day Durodhana's warriors gained more and more ground and Yudishtira's soldiers, worn out and tired of fighting, began to turn their backs on the enemy and flee.

Then Krishna, who was driving Arjuna's chariot, said to Arjuna: "Now the time has come to use the bow Gandiva." He took up the bow, and the arrows that came from it were like fiery flashes of lightning. Where they struck, not one but hundreds of enemy warriors fell down. And before the terror of the bow Gandiva, the soldiers of Durodhana turned away in fear and trembling and fled.

Durodhana himself tried to escape when he saw his soldiers running away. He hid in a river, hoping the brothers would not find him. But Natiala and Sahadeva, the fast riders, had followed his flight, and they told the other brothers where Durodhana was hidden.

Soon all five brothers came to the river and the strong Bishma challenged him to come out and fight him alone. Dripping with water, Durodhana emerged, fierce and full of hatred. He was armed with a mace, like Bishma, and the two warriors struck each other terrible blows. In the end a powerful blow by Bishma brought Durodhana down and the evil king, whose greed and envy had brought so much misery and suffering, was dead.

The old blind king, Durodhana's father, was deep in sorrow about all that had happened. He gave the crown of the whole kingdom to Yudishtira, to whom it really belonged. Then the blind king went into the forest alone and there he died. The sons of Pandu had, at last, regained their kingdom.

The Search for the Gate of Heaven

After the terrible battle on the plains of Kurukshetra, Yudishtira became king and ruler. He and his brothers ruled the country with great wisdom and justice for thirty five years. But then, however, the five brothers and Queen Draupadi were no longer young. It is quite hard work being king of a great country, and Yudishtira thought it was time for a younger man to take over. So he made one of Draupadi and Arjuna's sons the king.

Now that the brothers and Draupadi had given up their power and responsibilities, they could have enjoyed a pleasant, easy life without any more hard work. But they wanted something else, something that could only be found if they left behind all treasures, servants and comforts, and went up into the Himalaya mountains. For it was said that somewhere in the mountains there was a place where there was a gate which was the entrance to heaven. But it was also said that only those who had never been untruthful, conceited, afraid or unkind could find that gate and enter through it into heaven.

So the five brothers and Queen Draupadi left their splendid palaces and gardens and many servants behind and set out to seek the Gate of Heaven. They travelled without luggage or possessions, but Yudishtira did take his dog with him. It had been his companion for many years and he did not want to leave it at the palace.

Great were the hardships that they suffered in the cold, barren rocks of the Himalayas. Time passed as they searched and wandered on and on, but they had still not found the secret place of the Gate of Heaven. The hardships became too much for Queen Draupadi. She could go no further, and she lay down and died.

Draupadi's death made the brothers very sad but they went on with their journey. Saddest of all was Arjuna and his sorrow weakened him. There came a day when his legs would carry him no longer and, when he sat down, his brave heart stopped beating. Then Natiala and Sahadeva, the twins, who had always done things together and never been separated, became too weak to go on. And they too died.

Now only the strong Bishma, Yudishtira and the little dog were left. But even Bishma was not strong enough for the terrible hardships among the icy rocks of the Himalayas and, one morning, Yudishtira found his last brother dead. Yudishtira wondered how he, who was not the strongest but the weakest of the brothers, could go on when all the others had died before him.

But the next day as Yudishtira and his dog travelled on, a gate that seemed to be made of sunlight appeared before him. At the gate stood the god Indra, who called out: "Welcome, Yudishtira, you are the only one of the brothers who is without fault. Therefore only you have been allowed to find the gate. Come and enter the heavenly city of the gods!" But Yudishtira answered: "I will not enter through this gate without my brothers and Draupadi. All the glory of heaven means nothing to me without them." Then Indra smiled and said: "Come, Yudishtira, and meet your brothers and Draupadi in the heavenly city, for they have arrived before you."

But as Yudishtira approached the gate with his little dog following, Indra said: "Surely you don't think you can bring that dog with you! The dog is not allowed to enter." Yudishtira turned away and answered: "This dog has been faithful to me for many years, and I shall be faithful to him.

I will not leave him and if he cannot come with me, I will not enter the holy city of the gods."

When he had said these words, the dog changed before his eyes and became a god shining with light. And the god said: "1 am the God of justice and Fairness. Even though I appeared to you as a dog, you have remained faithful to me. For this you shall have greater honour in the heavenly city than any other man."

But the gods still had one more test in store for Yudishtira. When he entered into the heavenly city, where the gods dwelled in their glory, he could not see his brothers or Draupadi. He cried out: "Where are they?" Suddenly, he was no longer in the city of light but in a place of darkness where human voices cried out in pain. Among the voices, Yudishtira recognised those of his brothers and Draupadi. And he called out: "If you gods have done such a mean thing and condemned my brothers to stay in darkness and pain, then I do not want to be in the heavenly city. I shall stay with my brothers!"

When he said this the darkness was gone. He was in the city of light and his brothers and Draupadi were with him. And the great gods themselves, Brahma, Vishnu and Shiva, praised him as the most faithful and noble of all human souls in the holy city of the gods.

The Hermit and the Elephant

We have come to the end of the story of the five sons of Pandu. You remember that this story is really a very long poem in the Indian language. But you have heard only the most important parts of it because the poem itself is very, very long.

Now, the Indian language, in which this poem is still told, is a very interesting language. You see, just as children are younger than their parents, so the English, German, French and Russian languages which people speak today are really young languages. They are the 'children' of old languages. And the language in which the story of the sons of Pandu was told is a very old language. It is so old that it is not the mother but the grandmother language of English, and also of Russian, German and French.

Just as children look like their parents, and sometimes there is even a likeness to the grandparents, so there is a likeness between some words (not all, of course) in our language and the old language of India. For instance, the Indian word *duhitar* means daughter; *suna* means son; *pitar* is father, and mater is mother. *Brutar* means brother and *swasar* is sister.

And as children come from parents, so our word mother comes from the old word *matar*. Both the German word *mutter* and the French word mere also come from *matar*. Now, that ancient language of India is called Sanskrit and all the names you heard in the story of the sons of Pandu (like Indra, Yudishtira, Arjuna) are all names in Sanskrit, the grandmother of many languages which are spoken today.

Now you remember from many of the stories you have heard, quite often men left their homes and families and went to live as hermits in the forest. They had to live under great hardship, and although they did not do any work, they gave all their time to prayer. However, when these hermits prayed it was really quite hard work. For hours and hours every day a hermit would concentrate his mind on the words of a prayer, so that the whole world around him was forgotten. He would not feel heat, or cold, or rain. He would not feel hunger or thirst. As long as he prayed, his mind was on the prayer and nothing else.

It was this complete concentration on one task, so that nothing else entered the mind, which gave these hermits strange powers. It was not just prayer, but this deep concentration on the words of prayer, which gave them the strange power you have heard about in some of the stories. And even today there are hermits in India who still have these powers.

Now I want to tell you a story about such a modern-day hermit, a story about something that a man who had lived in India for many years saw with his own eyes. This man was staying in a small village on the edge of the forest. One day a hermit came out of the forest and squatted down in the road that went through the village. He was a strange sight as he sat there on the ground. He had a long black beard, shoulder-length hair and he was dressed only in a piece of rough cloth round his hips.

Most of the time his eyes were closed and he took no notice of what was going on around him. The villagers, the Indian peasants, treated him with great reverence. They walked carefully around the holy man and, from time to time, they would put a bowl of milk or a bowl with a little rice beside him. And so this hermit stayed squatting in the road, not speaking to anybody for many days.

Now the wild animals that live in the forests of India-the tigers, elephants, snakes and monkeys - usually stay away from the villages where people live because they don't like the smell of human beings. But there are exceptions. You know that elephants live in herds, like cows. And the elephants which belong to the same herd help each other when there is any danger. But sometimes it happens that there is one elephant who misbehaves. This mischief-maker starts kicking or hurting the other elephants with his tusks, or pushes them away when they go to drink at the river.

But eventually, the other elephants decide they have had enough of it, and the whole herd turns against him. They attack that naughty elephant, and they would throw him down and trample him to death if he did not run away. But he can never come back to the herd. Such an elephant, who has been driven away from his own herd, is called a rogue elephant. And once a rogue elephant knows he cannot come back to the herd, he goes mad with fury. He runs through the forest trumpeting wildly and trampling down everything that gets in the way. Even tigers flee before such a mad rogue elephant.

Now one morning, the people of that village were just leaving their huts to go to work in the fields. As the children came out in the road to play, the terribly loud trumpeting of an angry elephant could be heard. Then an enormous rogue elephant, his little eyes red with fury, came out of the forest and charged down the road. The people ran like mad, and scattered in all directions to get out of the way. Mothers snatched up their children and took them to safety, but a little toddler was still left in the road as the big elephant came charging down it.

In the excitement no one had paid attention to the hermit. But now he stood up, walked calmly into the middle of the road and stood there quietly, just in front of the child. The elephant kept charging but quite suddenly stopped three feet from the hermit. The holy man did not move at all, he only looked at the elephant.

For a few moments the peasants all held their breath while the elephant and the holy man looked at each other. Then the elephant turned away. All the wildness had gone out of him, and he walked quietly and tamely back into the forest. And the hermit sat down in the road again as if nothing had happened.

Rama and Hanuman

The Slaying of the Demons
In the next story you are going to hear there is much talk about evil spirits; spirits which can change their shape and simply delight in bringing harm to people. The Indian storytellers call these wicked spirits *rakshasas* but we shall call them demons, which is the name that is used in most tales from other countries.

There was a time, long ago, when these demons became terribly powerful in India. The Brahmins in their prayers, the peasants in their work, and the warriors in their training were never safe from attack. So the people of India begged the gods to put an end to these evil powers.

All the gods came to Brahma, the highest, and said: "Why is it that you let the demons have it all their own way. Are we, the good gods, not here to protect the earth?" But Brahma answered: "The king of the demons, Ravana, once, in times long past, earned a favour from me. The favour was that no god or other spirit should ever overcome or kill him. So none of you may fight against him."

The gods were greatly dismayed about this and cried: "But if no god or spirit can fight against Ravana, who can stop all the evil which is going on in the world?" And Brahma answered: "The wicked Ravana asked only that neither gods nor spirits harmed him but, in his pride, he did not mention human beings. Ravana thinks human beings are weak and miserable creatures. Yet it is from among them that a hero will be born who will, after a great struggle, make an end of Ravana. And the time is near when this human hero will be born."

Soon after, the hero, whose coming Brahma had promised, was born as the son of a great and powerful *rajah* or king. He was called Rama, and he had four older brothers. But Prince Rama's brothers could not match him fighting with spear, or bow and arrow, in riding horses and elephants, or in the knowledge of the holy poems which they all had to learn.

When Rama was only sixteen years old, a holy man, a Brahmin, came to his father and said: "O king, for many years I have lived in the forest trying to please the gods by constant prayer and sacrifices. But I cannot go on with my work for demons, sent by their king, Ravana, disturb my prayers and spoil my sacrifices by throwing dirt into the fire. I have heard people praise your son, Rama, as one of strength and courage. Let him come with me and drive out the demons."

Although the king was not happy to send such a young boy to fight the demons, he did not refuse the Brahmin. So Rama and one brother, Lakshman, who was very fond of him, went with the Brahmin into the forest.

They had hardly arrived when the demons appeared. Some had tigers' heads but birds' wings, while others had faces like men but the bodies of snakes. And there were others yet again who had ten arms and horns on their heads. From up in the air and down on the ground that horrible crowd came croaking, howling and yelling, so that even brave men might have taken fright. But not Rama and his faithful brother Lakshman. With sword in hand, he went to meet the monsters. He hit right and left and where he struck, a demon fell. Instead of frightening him, the monsters got a fright. Soon they turned and fled, and hurried back to their master, Ravana, to tell him what had happened.

When he had put the demons to flight, Rama asked the Brahmin if there was anything else he could do for him. "No," said the holy man, "but I am very grateful to you and I think I know of another task which is much more pleasant than fighting demons and monsters. I would like you to come with me to see the king of Janaka. He has a bow which no one has ever been able to bend, and he will give his daughter to the man who can bend it."

So Rama and his brother Lakshman went with the Brahmin to the land of Janaka. And when the prince saw Sita, the king's daughter, he was very happy for he had never seen a lady of such beauty. Eagerly, Rama took that great heavy bow and pulled the string. It began to bend, more and more, until there was a crack that was like thunder and the bow snapped and broke.

The king of Janaka, the father of the beautiful Sita, was very pleased for he could not wish for a better son-in-law than Rama, the prince and son of a great *rajah* himself. And so a great wedding was celebrated. Then Rama and his bride travelled back to his father who was overjoyed that his son had defeated the demons and gained such a noble and beautiful bride. But their happiness was not to last very long.

Rama's mother had died when he was still very young and his father had married another woman. Now this queen, the stepmother of Rama, had a son called Bharata. She wanted her son to become king, one day, rather than Rama.

When the stepmother heard that the old king was going to announce to the whole country that Rama, the best of his sons, would be king after him, she nearly burst with envy. She went to the king and said: "I want to remind you of something you promised me some years ago. You remember the great battle you fought against the enemies which had invaded our country. You were struck by an arrow, and your soldiers thought you were dead. When I heard the news, I rushed to the battlefield and found you; I took out the arrow and dressed your wound, and so I saved your life. And at that time you said you would grant me two wishes. All these years I have not asked any special favours, but now I am asking."

The king thought for a moment then he answered: "It is true, I did promise and I shall never break a promise I have made." The stepmother smiled and said: "Listen, these are my two wishes. I want my son, Bharata, to be announced as the future king. And I want Rama to be sent away to live in the forest for fourteen years."

That was a hard blow for the king, who loved Rama, but he could not break the promise he had made. When the stepmother had left, he called Rama and told him what had happened. But Rama was not at all disappointed or angry. He said: "A king must be true to his promise, and I would sooner go to the forest than make trouble for anybody in my family. Don't be sad, father, I am quite content to live for fourteen years in the forest."

However the stepbrother, Bharata, for whom the mother had done all this, also loved Rama. When he heard what had happened, he hastened to tell Rama that he had not known about his mother's plan, nor did he wish to take Rama's place. But the prince said: "I am not cross with you or your mother. My father's promise must be kept. I shall go to the forest."

Although Rama planned to spend those fourteen years alone, Sita would not part from him. So she too left the palace and came to share the hard life in the jungle. But if she had known what was in store for her, she may well have preferred to let Rama go alone.

Hanuman Comes to the Rescue

Rama, Sita, and Lakshman, the faithful brother, went deep into the forest where they had no company other than the animals of the jungle.

Most animals who live in the jungle keep away from human beings, but not the monkeys. Monkeys like to imitate people and the monkeys in the forest where Rama, Sita and Lakshman lived often came down from the trees and jumped about. In time Rama and Sita became great friends with them and even understood their language. And this friendship was to be a great blessing to Rama.

It happened like this. You remember that the king of the demons, Ravana, who could not be killed by gods or spirits, had sworn to revenge the demons Rama had killed. Now that Rama was in the forest, the demon king decided the right time had come. One of his spirits took on the shape of a deer with a coat the colour of gold. Of course there were many deer in the forest, but when the golden deer walked among the deep green plants and trees it was as if a golden moon was shining between the leaves.

When Rama saw the deer he thought: "What a wonderful gift a golden deer skin would be for Sita! She no longer has the rich robes of a princess. She has to dress in animal skins, but the skin of this deer is more beautiful than the finest silk!" He hurried back to the hut they had built to fetch his bow and arrow. Before he left he said to his brother Lakshman: "I am going to hunt a wonderful golden deer. You stay here and watch over Sita. Whatever happens, you must not leave her until I return."

So Rama went after the golden deer. Yet whenever he came near enough to shoot his arrow, the animal made a sudden leap and ran away. Little by little, Rama was led further and further away from the hut until he was many miles away deep in the forest.

Then the demon-in-the-deer made the mistake of waiting just too long before making another leap. Quick as lightning came the arrow, and struck. Before Rama's eyes the golden deer changed into a monster with the head of a crocodile and the body of a great snake. It lay dying on the ground but suddenly, with its last breath, the demon cried out in Rama's own voice: "Help! Lakshman, help!" so loudly that it could be heard far away in the hut. Then the monster died.

When Lakshman heard that terrible cry in his brother's voice, he forgot his promise, snatched up his bow and arrow, and ran out into the forest. But as soon as he had gone to try and find his brother, a hermit came to the hut. Sita, who knew that holy men should be treated with great respect, invited him to come in. However, the hermit was none other than Ravana, the king of the demons, who had cunningly changed into a human shape.

When Sita put a bowl of milk before the hermit, he looked at her with a strange smile and said: "Beautiful lady would you like to come with me?" – "What do you mean?" asked Sita, astonished. "I would never leave my husband, the noble Rama." – "Oh, yes you will," said the hermit, and he changed before her eyes. To her horror, she saw in place of the hermit a monster with ten heads growing from its neck, and twenty arms which reached out to grab her. She was dragged out of the hut and into a chariot, drawn by winged donkeys, that was waiting outside. As soon as they were both in the chariot, the donkeys spread their wings and the chariot soared high above the jungle. Sita, in her despair, took a veil she was wearing and threw it out of the chariot. In the jungle below, five monkeys on a mountain peak saw

Ravana's chariot up in the sky and picked up the veil that floated down from it.

Meanwhile Rama was on his way back from killing the golden deer which, as it turned out, was really a demon. When he saw Lakshman coming through the jungle, he wondered why his brother had left Sita alone in the hut. What was Lakshman doing in the forest, he wondered. Rama's heart was filled with fear and they both hurried back. But when they arrived, the hut was empty. Rama did not know where Sita had gone or what had happened to her.

Both Rama and his brother were in despair. They left the hut and began to search everywhere in the forest for some trace of Sita. At long last they came to the mountains and found the five monkeys who had caught Sita's veil. The monkeys told them that it was Ravana, the demon king, who had carried her away. But where had Ravana taken her? And how could Rama and his brother fight alone against the demon king who had thousands of horrible monsters and evil spirits as servants and warriors? It seemed as if there was no hope for Rama ever to see the beautiful Sita again. But then the five monkeys said: "Come with us to the king of all monkeys. If he is willing to help you then thousands and thousands of monkeys in all the forests of India will be on your side."

So Rama and his brother followed the monkeys to a great cave. Inside was a very big monkey with white hair and a clever look in his eyes. This was the king of all monkeys and, when he had heard the story, he said: "I and all my people will help, and you shall have an army of monkeys to fight on your side. I am too old to take part in the war against the demons, but I will give you the strongest, fastest and most cunning of my monkeys to lead the army and do everything you want him to do. His name is Hanuman."

At the command of their king, hundreds of thousands of monkeys came pouring out of all the forests of India. Their leader, Hanuman, was not only strong and clever but he also had magic powers. And Hanuman told the monkeys: "Go out all over the mountains and forests of India and seek everywhere for Sita, the wife of Rama."

Hanuman, himself, also searched for her. When he came to the sea-shore, he heard people talk about an island far across the water where neither fishermen or sailors would land because it was inhabited by evil monsters. And he thought: "Surely, this must be the stronghold of Ravana." There was no ship that would take him across, so Hanuman called on the gods to help him. Then he took a mighty leap, high up, and in one great jump landed on the island.

The island was surrounded on all sides by a great wall, but he jumped over it easily and found himself in a beautiful garden with flowers and fruit trees. Hanuman quickly jumped up a fruit tree and waited. At first he saw only demons with horns or long ears on their several heads but they took no notice of him. Then he saw a human being, a woman with a beautiful but sad face.

Hanuman knew that this must be Sita. As she walked under the tree, he whispered to her: "Sita, I am a messenger from your husband, Rama. Be of good cheer for you will soon be free." Sita looked up at him and smiled at the good news. But the demons had seen her stop and listen to the monkey and, before Hanuman could make one of his great leaps, he was caught, pulled down and dragged before Ravana.

The Monkey Army Goes to Battle

The demons had caught Hanuman and, shouting with joy, they dragged their prisoner into the great palace where the dreadful Ravana had his court. Sita was also pushed before the throne of Ravana. When the demon king saw the monkey, his ten faces lit up with grim smiles. And one head, which looked like a vulture, said: "I have no doubt that this monkey is a spy sent by Rama. But we shall deal with that spy! Bring me a burning torch. I will set fire to the monkey's tail."

When Sita heard what Ravana planned to do to the poor monkey, who had come for her sake, her heart was full of grief and pity. Silently she prayed to the fire and said: "As I am faithful to my husband Rama, so you, fire, be cool to the tail of Hanuman and do not hurt him!"

By now a demon-servant had brought a burning torch to Ravana. He took the torch, and all the demons laughed with delight as he put it to the monkey's tail. The bushy end of Hanuman's tail immediately caught fire. But Sita's prayer had been heard. Hanuman felt no pain and, although his tail was in flames, not a single hair was even singed.

However, the flames and sparks frightened the two demons who were holding Hanuman by the arms and they let go. No longer in the grip of the demons, the monkey made one great leap through an open window and was outside. His next leap was up to the roof of the palace where he touched the wooden rafters with his burning tail. In a moment the roof and the whole palace was on fire.

Shouting and yelling, Ravana and his demons came pouring out of the burning palace but the faithful monkey did not flee. He stayed on the roof until he could see that Sita had also escaped from the flames. Then Hanuman made another one of his great leaps. Just as the burning roof collapsed under him, he jumped off right into the sea where the water quenched the fire on his tail. Yet not a hair of it had been damaged. The monkey climbed on to a rock on the shore and took yet another great leap across the sea to India. Then he hurried back to tell Rama that he had found Sita imprisoned on the island of demons.

Rama praised Hanuman for having served him so faithfully. Now that they knew where Sita was, the vast army of monkeys made themselves ready for the great battle against Ravana and his demons. And it was such a sight to see Rama, Lakshman and Hanuman leading an army of hundreds of thousands of monkeys. The soldiers in that army did not march in line; they skipped and jumped and they climbed trees and hung from the branches by their tails. But for all their jumping and leaping, they still moved swiftly down to the sea.

Now Rama had no ships to carry his great army, and only Hanuman could jump as far as the island of demons. So Rama called on the God of the Ocean to come and help him. In answer to his prayer the waters began to churn, as if the whole sea was boiling. At last, out of the foam, an enormous green head appeared with hair and a beard of sea-weed.

It was the Ocean God and he said: "Every element has its own law, and the law of the ocean waters is that they cannot stand still and that they are a fathomless deep. I cannot stop the waters for you and I cannot make the sea dry, but I can do one thing for you: I will command the waves to carry anything – stones, rocks, earth, grass or sand – as if it were wood and it shall not sink. Tell your monkeys to build a pathway of stones across the water and it will hold." Having said this, the Ocean God sank down again to the depths from where he had come, and which no man has ever seen.

On Rama's command the monkeys set to work. There was no more skipping and jumping for now there was real work to be done, and it had to be done quickly before Ravana and his demons could come and interfere. So hundreds of thousands of monkeys carried rocks and stones and sand and earth. And as they threw them into the water they did not sink but stayed on the surface to form a narrow bridge.

On the morning of the third day, Ravana, the demon king, saw a great host of monkeys pouring over the bridge towards his island fortress. There were so many he could not even count them and the noise they made was like the sound of a hundred waterfalls. But the demon king did not, for a moment, think he was beaten. He had a mighty army of demons and monsters, and now he called on them to drive off the invading monkeys. The brave monkeys advanced, scaling the walls and fighting against the demons with stones, rocks and heavy sticks. But the demons fought back with claws and sharp teeth, and some of them had many arms to fight with.

The air was filled with terrible noise and the ground was soon covered with the corpses of demons and monkeys. The sea around the island turned red with the blood spilled in the fighting. During the day the monkeys kept the upper hand and killed many of the monsters. But at night time, when demons are strongest, they not only killed thousands of monkeys but they fell down upon the dead and devoured them.

But the following morning Rama, Lakshman and Hanuman joined the battle and, where they fought, the demons were scattered like leaves in a storm. Ravana, the demon king, began to fear that he would lose and he thought: "Things are looking black for me, I must get the help of my brother."

Ravana's brother, who had the strange name Khumba (which means 'pot') was the largest giant among the demons. But he was also the laziest. Khumba would sleep for ten months on end, then, when he woke up, he would eat and eat and gorge himself until he could eat no more. Then he would lie back and sleep again. Yet, if he could be roused, he was the largest and the most terrible fighter. Khumba had been asleep for nine months now in a huge deep cave. He lay snoring in his cellar and not even all the noise from the battle could rouse him. But Ravana decided he was going to wake Khumba up.

Rama's Magic Arrow
Ravana and a host of his demons made their way to the cave where Khumba was asleep. He was lying there like a mountain, and the breath that came from his open mouth was like a gale. The demons made ready great heaps of meat, piled up as high as houses, and great jars of blood for him to drink. Then they started to blow trumpets, beat drums and to shout and roar. They made such a noise that the birds that flew over the cave fell down dead with fright. But Khumba still slept on.

Then the demons took wooden sticks and hit the sleeping giant. Others took boiling hot water and poured it over him or yelled into his ears. But Khumba was still asleep. At last Ravana had elephants brought in and, after they were driven over the giant, he began to blink his eyes. Then he yawned, and all the elephants rushed away in fear from the storm that came from his mouth.

When Khumba, the laziest of all demons, sat up, he

saw the hills of meat and the buckets of blood waiting for him. He fell to and ate and drank until nothing was left. When he had finished he put his head down again, ready to take another ten months rest. But Ravana and the other demons shouted at him. They told him what had happened and asked for his help. Then Khumba said: "Well, I am going to have a feast of monkey meat, and I am going to eat Rama and Lakshman as well." He got up and he was like a walking mountain.

When Khumba walked into the raging battle, even the brave monkeys were struck with terror. With his large paws he would grab a fistful of monkeys, twenty or thirty at a time, and put them in his mouth and swallow them. Rama saw the giant monster and he fired an arrow from his bow that cut off Khumba's right arm. The next arrow sliced through his left arm, and the third cut off his head. Then the body fell with a great crash into the sea.

But when Ravana saw his giant brother slain, he mounted his own battle-chariot and drove out to fight Rama and revenge his brother. He took a magic arrow and aimed it at Rama. Every one of Ravana's arrows changed as it flew through the air. One arrow head became a tiger's head ready to bite, another became a snake's head with poisoned fangs, while yet a third became a red flame ready to burn Rama.

But Rama, too, had magic arrows and his became golden rays of sunshine and glittering stars. They met Ravana's arrows midway and the demon's arrows fell powerless to the ground. Then Rama shot arrows that were like lightning and they cut off one after another of the demon king's heads. But as quickly as they were cut off, other heads grew in their place.

Finally, Rama took one arrow from his quiver and he spoke over that arrow a single magic word that was known only to himself. Then he put the arrow on the bow and let it fly. It struck Ravana, the demon king, in the heart and he fell to the ground and died. Neither god, nor spirit could kill Ravana but Rama, the man, had slain him with the power of a secret word. And after Ravana had fallen, the demons all fled in despair. They left the island, and never again did they have the power they had possessed when Ravana was king.

Sita came out of the prison where she had been held, and both she and Rama were very happy to be together again. They were deeply grateful for the wonderful help they had been given by the monkeys. Then Rama said to Hanuman: "From now on all people, wherever they are, who remember the great battle against Ravana shall never hurt or harm any monkey." To this day, people in India hold monkeys sacred and would not hurt them in any way.

By that time the fourteen years which Rama had to stay away from his kingdom had also passed. So he and Sita and the faithful Lakshman returned. Meanwhile, Rama's father had died and his stepbrother had become king. But as soon as they arrived the stepbrother met Rama with joy and gave the crown and throne to him.

Rama and Sita ruled for many years. As long as they lived no one in the kingdom ever committed any crime. There were no thieves, murderers, liars or cheats in Rama's kingdom. When Rama and Sita died they were received as companions of the gods in heaven. And people in India pray to Rama and Sita, even today.

Buddha, the Enlightened One

The Gentle Prince Sidhartha
In the story of Rama you heard of a great hero who conquered evil spirits in battle. But now I want to tell you the story of a gentle man who never killed or harmed any other being in his life. And this man was as great a hero as Rama.

Now at that time in ancient India warriors were brave in war and strong in battle. And even though kings ruled their people with wisdom and with justice, there was one thing missing. This was compassion or mercy. For instance when a warrior saw an enemy lying wounded on the battlefield, he would kill the wounded man rather than spare his life. And if a man was hungry or even starving, a stranger would not help him or give him food. People were brave or cowardly, they were truthful or untruthful, they were just or unjust. But they were not kind or gentle. They had no pity when they saw others suffer.

In the heavenly city where the gods dwell, a soul came before Brahma, Vishnu and Shiva and said: "1 want to teach men on earth pity and compassion, for they are cruel and heartless and they don't even know they are cruel." And Brahma answered: "Only a very special soul can become a teacher of kindness and pity. Only when you have lived not once but many times; only when you have suffered every pain and every sorrow which people can suffer; only then can you become such a teacher. The name for such a teacher is Buddha. It will take many lives on earth in hardship and sorrow and suffering to become a Buddha, a teacher of compassion and mercy. Are you willing to take this upon yourself?" And the soul answered: "Yes I will."

In time the soul who wanted to become a Buddha was born on earth. He became a king and even though his land was taken from him by an enemy, the king felt no hatred for his enemy. Nor did he want revenge. He died in great poverty but soon after he was born again as a peasant. He married and had many children and he loved them with all his heart. But there was a war and foreign soldiers took the children and sold them as slaves. The peasant never saw them again, yet he did not allow himself to hate the soldiers who had taken his children. And so he died.

Once again the soul returned: this time as the child of poor parents. When he was still very young, his parents died in an epidemic. But no one wanted to look after or give food to a little orphan. The child lived on grains which people had left in the fields, but he never allowed himself to hate those who drove him away when he begged for food.

So the soul who wanted to become a Buddha lived life after life on earth. He was born again and again, and in every life he had to suffer. But he never felt hatred or wished for revenge on those who had caused his suffering. At last the time came when that soul left the earth and appeared before Brahma. The god spoke to him and said: "You have now learnt all you had to learn to become a Buddha, a teacher of mercy and compassion. In your next life on earth you will be a Buddha and, when you return to heaven, you will be higher than the gods. Even we, the gods, bow before a Buddha."

Living in India at that time was a king whose name was Suddhodana. His wife, the queen, was called Maya and one night she had a dream. She saw herself surrounded by a vast crowd of people who all bowed down before her. When she told the dream to King Suddhodana, he called the wisest men of his kingdom to tell him what it meant. The wise men held a council and when they had spoken amongst themselves, the oldest of them said: "Rejoice, Queen Maya. You will have a son who will be great among men."

The wise man continued: "But your son will have the choice between two kinds of greatness. If he stays here at the court of King Suddhodana, he will become a mighty ruler. His conquests shall reach the farthest corners of the earth, and many nations will call him their lord and master. But he can also do something else; he can forsake his throne. He could renounce the glory, fame and treasures and become a humble beggar. If he does that he will be a great teacher. He will become a Buddha which means 'one whose mind is filled with the light of the highest wisdom' or 'the enlightened one'."

When the king heard this he was very pleased that his future son would, in any case, be a great and famous man. But Suddhodana also decided that he would do everything possible to make sure he was a mighty ruler rather than a homeless beggar.

In time Queen Maya gave birth. And, although she did not know it, in that child was the soul which had gone through so much suffering in earlier lives in order to become a Buddha. The boy was called Sidhartha and he was taught all the things a king's son had to learn, like how to drive a chariot and use a bow and arrow.

Yet Sidhartha did not behave as other princes did. Sometimes in a chariot race, when his horses were well ahead of the other contestants, the prince would deliberately stop and let others win. He found little pleasure in making his horses run any further when he saw the animals were sweating and breathing hard under the strain.

And although Sidhartha's arrows never missed their mark when the target was a piece of wood, the prince refused to go hunting and try his skill on living animals. The other young men of noble birth at the court often laughed about their future king who would not hunt the animals of the forest. But Sidhartha paid no attention to their laughter.

One of the young men at the court of Suddhodana was Prince Sidhartha's cousin, Devadatta. He was very proud of his skill with bow and arrow and was always ready to practice on any animal he saw. One day Devadatta was in the palace garden when a flock of wild swans flew overhead. Thinking that the white birds against the blue sky made a wonderful target, he quickly took out his bow and arrow. He sent a shaft up to the flying birds and the arrow caught the wing of a swan. The bird flew slower and slower, then it fluttered down in another part of the gardens and it fell near Prince Sidhartha.

Blood flowed from the wing as the prince picked the swan up. At first the swan hissed and seemed fierce, but a mere stroke of Sidhartha's hand soothed the bird. He took out the barb of the arrow and put some ointment on the wound. Then a servant came and said: "My master, Prince Devadatta, shot a swan and he saw it come down somewhere in this part of the gardens. Have you, Prince Sidhartha, seen it?" Sidhartha replied: "Yes, this is the swan, but I am going to save its life and Devadatta cannot have it." When the servant delivered this message, Devadatta was very angry. He went to Sidhartha and demanded his swan back, but Sidhartha refused to let him have it.

In the end both princes agreed that their quarrel should be settled by the wise men of the court. When the wise men had heard the whole story they said: "Surely, he who saves the life of a living being has a better claim to it than one who only wants to kill." So Sidhartha looked after the swan until it was well enough to fly away. But from that time onwards Devadatta hated him.

Journeys beyond the Palace Wall
King Suddhodana, the father of the gentle and kind Prince Sidhartha, did not wish his son to become anything other than a great warrior who would conquer many nations. He certainly did not want his son to become a Buddha who would live as a homeless beggar.

So he asked the wise men of his court: "What can I do to be sure that my son will become a great king rather than a teacher who will live in poverty?" The wise men told him: "The prince is still young; upto now he has lived in a beautiful palace with splendid gardens. He has not seen poverty. He has not seen any old or sick people. He has not seen the death of any person or a dead body. And, if you want to keep him, it must go on like this; he must not see old age, suffering, illness or death. If he sees any of these things he will surely leave you."

Now King Suddhodana did everything in his power to make it impossible for his son to see anything sad or anyone who was suffering. Only young, healthy, beautiful people were allowed in the court. Around the palace the king built not one but three high walls so that the prince should not, by chance, catch a glimpse of death or illness among the people outside. Inside the walls, in the palace and the garden, there was every possible entertainment and pleasure for the prince; games, plays, music and sports. But no one was allowed to mention illness, death or sorrow in his presence.

Sidhartha seemed well content with this pleasant life. When he became older he married a beautiful princess. He was so happy that his father thought he need not worry about his son again. But one day the prince announced that he wanted to ride in his chariot beyond the palace walls and through the city. When King Suddhodana heard of this he immediately sent heralds into the city to say that when Prince Sidhartha drove through the streets no one who was old or sick must be visible. The king also commanded that no funerals take place and that people put on their best clothes and decorate every house with flowers.

The day came; Prince Sidhartha's chariot drove through the city. Beside the prince was Channa, his charioteer, who drove the horses. Wherever they went crowds of young healthy people stood in the streets. But as the chariot turned a corner, an old man suddenly tottered right in front of it. No one knew how he came to be there, and people later said it was one of the gods who had taken human form. But whoever it was, it was an old man bent with age, with white hair, wrinkled skin and eyes that were dim.

Then Sidhartha asked: "What happened to this man that he is so different from the others?" The chariot driver could only answer truthfully: "That is an old man. All human beings get like that when they have lived for a long time." When the prince heard this he ordered the charioteer to drive back to the palace. He could no longer enjoy the gardens, the amusements and pleasures. For many days he was in deep thought, but after a while he forgot the old man and lived as before.

Some time later Sidhartha went for another drive in his chariot with Channa beside him. The crowds in the streets were all young and healthy for, again, the king's heralds had decreed that no old or sick person was allowed to come out on this day. As they passed through the city, Prince Sidhartha saw only men and women who were young and strong like himself. But once again something happened against the king's command. Just as the chariot passed by, a man appeared on the pavement. His face was pale, his skin was covered with a rash, his hands trembled and he could only walk by holding himself up with a stick. No one knew who he was, no one knew where he had come from and no-one knew where he went afterwards.

When Prince Sidhartha saw the pitiful figure he asked the charioteer: "What's the matter with this man?" And the charioteer answered: "He must be sick, he suffers from some illness." And Sidhartha said: "Sick, illness? What does it mean, I have never heard of it?" So the charioteer explained that any person can, at any time, fall sick; that no one is safe from illness. When the prince heard this he told the charioteer to drive back to the palace. He was sad. He could no longer enjoy the gardens and pleasures when he thought of how people suffered from all kinds of illness. Yet, after a while, he put it out of his mind. He forgot the sick man, just he had forgotten the old man.

A Meeting with Death
It was not often that Prince Sidhartha wanted to leave the beautiful palace and the pleasant company that was provided at the royal court. There was so much to keep him amused and occupied that there was little reason why he should want to go out into the city. But even the most

pleasant life can get boring if there is no change. So once again he made it known that he wanted to go for a drive. As soon as his father heard about it, heralds went out and warned the people that anyone old or sick in the streets that day would be severely punished.

But as the prince and his charioteer drove through the city, a strange procession appeared. A row of men and women walked in the middle of the street so slowly that Sidhartha's chariot had to stop. The men at the front of the procession carried on their shoulders a stretcher on which lay a human figure all wrapped up. Behind followed men and women who cried and sobbed. And no one knew who they were or where they had come from.

The prince looked at this strange spectacle and asked the charioteer: "Tell me, what is this? Why are the people crying? And why do we have to stop for them?" The charioteer answered: "My lord, what you see is a funeral." – "A funeral?" Asked Sidhartha. "What does that mean?" And the charioteer answered: "That figure on the stretcher is the body of a man who has died. The family of the dead man are taking his body to a place where it will be buried." And the prince asked: "A man who has died? What are you talking about? What has happened to that man?" So the charioteer explained to him that no human being can live forever. Everyone must die at some time; of old age or illness, in accidents or war. Everyone in the world must die some day.

Prince Sidhartha had never heard of death before. Now he realised that not only all the people in the city would die some time but also his friends, parents, brothers, sisters and he, himself. He felt so sad that he gave the order to drive back to the palace. And as Channa drove the chariot back through the streets, the prince recalled the old man and the sick man he had seen. But worst of all, he could not forget the dead man. From that day on, Prince Sidhartha felt he would never be happy again.

When he arrived at the palace, a servant came to tell him that his wife had given birth to a son. Sidhartha went to see her and the baby. All he could say was: "This makes it even harder," but his wife did not understand what he meant. That evening a great feast was held at the palace to celebrate the birth. There was music and merry-making, but the prince watched the celebrations very quietly. Late at night the feast came to an end, all the people went to bed and soon the whole palace was quiet.

When everybody was asleep Prince Sidhartha left his room. Softly he walked to the room where his wife and son were fast asleep. A dimmed lamp shed some light in the room and although he longed to touch his child, he did not want to wake the baby or the mother. After one long look, he turned and left. Then he called his faithful charioteer and told him to saddle the best horse. The driver was surprised that he wanted to go for a ride in the middle of the night. But Prince Sidhartha said: "I am going for my last ride. Tonight I am leaving my home and my family."

When the horse was ready, Sidhartha rode away carefully and slowly so that the clatter of the hooves would not disturb anybody. And by the power of the gods, the soldiers on guard at the palace gate were fast asleep and did not wake up when he passed. The faithful charioteer, Channa, accompanied the prince and they rode away from the palace and out of the city.

They had gone some distance before the prince stopped. He dismounted and changed his royal robes for the rough cloth worn by hermits. He gave the robes and the horse to the charioteer and told him to take them back to the palace and tell his family that he had left for good. And so began a new life for Sidhartha.

Sidhartha, the Homeless Beggar
Prince Sidhartha had left his royal home and all the pleasures and joys which his father had so carefully arranged for him. However, he had not left his family and little son for selfish reasons. That would have been quite wrong.

Because Sidhartha's heart was full of pity and compassion for all the suffering people in the world, he wanted to find a way of bringing some comfort and help to all those people. But in order to do that he had to give up his own happiness; he had to give up his family and his life of pleasure at the palace. And this is something you will find again and again in history; that great men and women, who have helped thousands of others, often had to give up or sacrifice their own happiness.

So Prince Sidhartha was no longer a prince but a homeless beggar. He was used to the choicest food but now he had to beg for things to eat. When he sat down for the first time on the roadside to eat what people had put into his bowl, bits of stale vegetables and bread or rice that had been cooked days before, he could hardly swallow. Then he said to himself: "This will be my food in future. I must get used to it." And he forced himself to eat whether he liked it or not.

But Sidhartha did not spend much time either collecting food or eating it. Most of the time he spent thinking about the question: "What can I do to help the many unhappy people in the world?" For a long time he could not find any answer.

Then other holy men he met told him that if he tried to go without food as long as possible, the gods would send an answer to his question. So Sidhartha went without food. He fasted for days on end and became so lean and haggard that no one would have recognised him. One day he fainted from sheer exhaustion. When he came to he said to himself: "Now I know that fasting is not the right way to find an answer to my question." And he again began to eat what people gave him.

But, although he did not yet know it, the time was near at hand when he should become Buddha, and all the suffering he had experienced in earlier lives on earth would bear fruit. One day, in the hot season, when the sun burnt down, Sidhartha came to the outskirts of a little village. He saw a great fig tree and sat down in its shade. As so often before, his mind turned to the great question: "What can I do to help the unhappy people in the world?"

But the evil spirits and demons knew that the time was near when Sidhartha would receive an answer and become a Buddha. So the king of the demons, Mara, called up thousands and thousands of monsters and spirits. The whole sky was darkened by a black cloud that was nothing but demons; demons with fiery tongues; demons with ten arms; demons with claws and fangs; demons like snakes and dragons. That whole vast army of demons swooped down on the lonely beggar under the fig tree,

Sidhartha, however, was deep in thought which was so powerful that it was like a rainbow around him; a rainbow through which no evil could penetrate. The demons hurled stones, spears and arrows at Sidhartha but all the weapons fell down powerlessly when they came to the rainbow. In desperation the demons threw themselves against the rainbow to break through. They clawed it, they hit it and they ran their heads against it, but it was as hard as diamond. And all that time Sidhartha did not take any notice of the swarm of monsters. He remained undisturbed and calm in his thoughts.

When Mara, the demon king, saw that his army of horrors could not harm Sidhartha he thought of another trick. He sent all his demons away. Then Mara, himself, took on the shape of a human being. He ran towards the tree and called out: "Prince Sidhartha, I have a message from your wife. Your little son is ill and may only live for a few days. Come quickly, perhaps when the child sees you he will recover." But Sidhartha answered: "All men must die sooner or later. I must find consolation for all sorrows, not only for my own or my wife's sorrow if our child should die."

Then Mara said: "Enemies have invaded your father's country. He needs the strong arm of his son, or he will lose his land and his life." But Sidhartha answered: "Kings have lost their land and life before. I must find consolation for all sorrows, not only for my father's." Mara then knew he was defeated. He went away, his power broken.

Enlightenment Under the Fig Tree
Once the evil demon, Mara, had been driven away, Sidhartha entered into deep concentrated thought, so that he was no longer aware of anything around him. Nor did he allow any feelings of hunger, thirst or tiredness to disturb his thinking. And what were his thoughts? They were really a question and the question was: "How can people become free of evil?"

A day and a night passed while Sidhartha sat asking with his whole heart and mind: "How can the soul free itself of evil?" By the end of the first night it was as if his mind had left the body, and he saw one of the great secrets of the world. He saw that the souls of human beings do not die when the body dies. They live for a while in a higher world, and then return to earth and are born again.

But for every evil deed, for every hurt they caused, for every untruth they told in one life, in the next life they must pay with unhappiness, sorrows, illness or pain. Then Sidhartha knew that the first step to become free of evil is to know that, one day, you have to pay for misdeeds, if not in this life then in the next.

Sidhartha was not satisfied with this answer, and his mind was still filled with the question: "How can the soul become free of evil?" He remained in deep thought, without food, drink or sleep, and so passed the second day and the second night. Then freed of the body, his mind saw the souls of men going from one earth life to the next and, in one way or another, paying for evil they had done. But now Sidhartha could actually see inside the souls. Now he could see what made people do evil things, such as hurt others by deeds or words or lies. He could see that behind all evil is selfishness.

Then Sidhartha knew that in order to be free of evil, the soul must understand that all evil comes from selfishness.

But Sidhartha was still not satisfied even with this second answer. So he remained in deep thought, without food, without drink, without sleep, for a third day and a third night. During the night his mind, freed of the body, soared up to great heights and he saw that all human souls had, long, long ago, come from one very great soul; the soul of all mankind. And just as many little drops can come from a great lake or many little sparks are born from one great fire, so Sidhartha saw that this great soul of mankind, from which we all come, was full of love. It was so full of compassion for every being in the world that there was no room for any selfishness.

When Sidhartha saw the glory of love and kindness that is the soul of all mankind, it was as if his mind was flooded with light. At last he knew the answer to his question: the soul becomes free of evil through love, kindness, compassion and pity; by caring more and more for others. Because it was like a wonderful inner light to know this, this experience of the third night is called enlightenment. And Sidhartha, who was the first to have such an experience, was from that time called 'the Enlightened One' or, in the Indian language, Buddha.

From that day onwards Sidhartha became known in India, and in later times all over the world, as Buddha, the great teacher of love and compassion who could show others how to become free of evil. But Sidhartha was only really preparing the way for the great soul of mankind that he had seen as he sat under the fig tree, to be born on earth five hundred years later as Jesus Christ. The rest of mankind had to wait for Jesus to come to earth, but Prince Sidhartha, the Buddha, saw him long before; on the third night, the night of enlightenment, which, it is said, was on the night of the full moon in May.

Krishna, a God in Disguise

King Kamsa's Cruel Deed
Do you remember that in the story of the sons of Pandu, a great and noble king helped Arjuna in the battle against Durodhana. This king, who was Arjuna's chariot driver, was called Krishna and it is the story of his life you will begin to hear today.

Yet the story of Krishna began long before he was born. It starts with another king, called Kamsa, who was very powerful. He had great armies and wonderful treasures, but all this made him very proud and conceited. He was also heartless and cruel and the people he ruled were very afraid of him. If, for instance, the king was in an evil mood he would burn a peasant's hut because the smell of the hut had offended him as he rode past.

But just as Kamsa was proud and cruel, his daughter Ashra was humble, gentle and kind. She was to be married to a prince and a great wedding feast was planned. Now it happened that when King Kamsa was on his way to the wedding, he saw a hermit sitting by the roadside. And the hermit said: "Great are you, King Kamsa, but the eighth child that will be born to your daughter will be greater than you, and it will even destroy you."

When Kamsa heard this he rushed to the great hall where all were ready for the wedding. He shouted at his daughter and her bridegroom that there was to be no wedding, for one of their future children would kill him. The daughter and the prince pleaded with him. They promised they would bring every child to him as soon as it was born, and he, King Kamsa, could decide if the child should live or be killed. And to this the king agreed.

In time the first child was born. As it was a girl Kamsa did not think it would be dangerous to him, and the baby was allowed to live. The next child was a boy. He did not look a strong baby, so he too was allowed to live. Eventually seven children were born to Ashra and each was allowed to live.

But Kamsa had not forgotten the prophecy. One day his spies came and told him that his daughter was expecting another baby, the eighth. Determined that the princess and her husband would not play any tricks on him, Kamsa ordered his soldiers to throw them both in prison. And day and night soldiers stood guard outside.

The princess and her husband were terribly unhappy. They saw no hope that the child could possibly live for more than a few hours after it had come into the world. So they both prayed to the gods, for only the gods could help them now. Then one night the prince, the father, saw in a dream the Thunder God, Indra, before him.

The god spoke to him and said: "The child that will be born to your wife will not be an ordinary man. One of the gods, Vishnu, himself, will be born as a human being in this child. Therefore fear not! When the child is born walk out of this prison and go down to the river where a poor man and his wife live. She will have a baby at the same time. You must leave your child with the poor people and return to the prison with theirs." When the prince woke he wondered how it would be possible to accomplish all the god Indra had said. Yet both he and his wife felt happier for they knew the gods were helping them.

The next night there was a great storm and, while the winds howled outside, the princess gave birth to a baby boy.

The wind was so loud that the soldiers could not hear the little one crying. But, stranger even, the soldiers on guard felt so tired that they could not stay awake and, one by one, they dropped to the ground and fell asleep. Then, before the astonished eyes of the prince and his wife, the prison door opened. They could have both fled, but they knew that King Kamsa's soldiers would easily catch them with the child the next day, and they obeyed Indra's command.

The princess stayed in the prison while the prince carried the child down to the poor man's hut by the river. The man and his wife were both asleep but beside the woman was her newborn child. The prince quickly put his own son down, took her child and hurried back to the prison. As soon as he was back the doors closed behind him.

In the morning the guards woke up, saw the new-born child, and brought the news to Kamsa. The evil king walked into the prison and, with his own sword, struck the child and killed it. Then he let the princess and prince go. Now King Kamsa felt safe, for he thought he had killed the eighth child of his daughter.

An Invitation to the Palace
Although the infant Krishna had escaped King Kamsa's sword, there were other threats to come. As the months went by many demons and evil spirits began to see that he was a child of more than human power. So they decided to destroy him while he was still young.

One day, a demon, disguised as a peasant woman, came to the poor man's hut and said to the mother (who was really only the foster-mother): "I have heard of the lovely baby boy you have got. Oh, what a sweet child! Why don't I look after him while you get on with your work."

The poor woman was very pleased with such a kind offer and left the visitor with the child in the hut. As soon as the demon woman was alone with the baby, she put her fingers round the child's throat to strangle it. But a searing fire came from the child and killed her. When the foster-mother returned she saw a half-burned dead monster, with a goat's head and a bird's body, lying beside the baby's cradle.

As Krishna grew older he used to go with the other boys to watch over herds of cows grazing on the hills. Again the demons tried to kill him. One waited as a poisonous snake, hidden in the grass. As the boy came nearer and nearer the snake rose up, ready to strike and bite. Suddenly Krishna jumped up, came down with his heel right on the snake's head and crushed it.

Another time a demon turned himself into a calf. Young Krishna was fond of calves. He used to come to play with them and would even climb on their backs. One day, he saw a black calf among the others and he climbed on to it. But then the black calf galloped away towards a cliff, so as to throw Krishna down to his death. At the last moment Krishna jumped lightly off the calf's back and gave it a kick that sent it over the edge, where it shattered on the rocks below. After that, the demons realized that they had no power to destroy the child.

When Krishna was older he became a real cowherd, and in that part of India cowherds all played a bamboo flute. Krishna too learnt to play, but no one had ever played the flute as he could play. People came from far and near to listen to him, and animals also loved the music. It was not only the cows who stopped chewing their cud and stood around him: foxes, wolves, tigers and deer stood peacefully, side by side, listening quietly. The monkeys stopped chattering and the birds came down from the trees to hear Krishna playing the flute. Of course people talked about the strange young cowherd and, in time, the evil King Kamsa came to hear of him. He felt a strange fear and wondered about this young man. Perhaps, after all, his daughter's eighth child was still alive? So the king decided to go in search of the hermit who had once spoken to him at the roadside.

When he found the old hermit, he said: "You are a holy man and you cannot tell a lie. So tell me, is my daughter's eighth child still alive?" The hermit had to answer: "Yes," but he also knew it was the will of the gods that Kamsa should know. Then Kamsa asked: "Is he the strange young cowherd they talk about?" Again the hermit said: "Yes."

Now King Kamsa knew the truth, his evil heart was full of anger and fury. But he thought a long time before he made up his mind what to do. Then he sent a message to the poor man and woman who were Krishna's foster-parents, inviting them and their son to attend a great tournament that was to be held at the royal court. King Kamsa's messenger, however, was a kind and good man. He had watched the king's face when he told him to invite Krishna and his parents, and he knew there were evil plans afoot. When he reached the hut by the river the messenger told Krishna: "I must obey the king's command to invite you but I warn you, don't go." Krishna smiled at him and said: "Do not fear for me. I shall go, but only my enemies will suffer." And so the foster-parents and Krishna set out for the tournament at the royal court.

Krishna becomes King

Although warned, Krishna had accepted evil King Kamsa's invitation to the tournament. There were great crowds waiting to watch the spectacle, but when Krishna arrived they all stared at him. No one had seen a more handsome young man, so tall and strong, and they all could feel he carried a kind of power that is not found in ordinary human beings. And they all whispered: "He is like a king, though he is dressed in a cowherd's garb?"

In the crowd was an old woman, ugly and hunchbacked, who had known little happiness in her life. As this old misshapen woman looked upon Krishna with awe and wonder, she sighed and thought to herself: "The gods must love this young man to make him such a fine-looking fellow. Perhaps they don't love me, and that's why they made me so ugly?"

Just then Krishna was passing close to her. He smiled and said, as if he could read her thoughts: "But you are not ugly, and the gods do love you." Then he bent down and kissed the woman on the forehead. And in this moment she was changed. Her hunchback disappeared, the wrinkles of age disappeared, her ugly features became beautiful, and she was transformed into a young and very lovely girl. All the people around who saw it happen gasped with astonishment, but Krishna walked on and went into the great field where the tournament was just about to begin.

First there was wrestling and the strongest men in the kingdom were there to compete for the prize: a golden cup that King Kamsa would present to the winner. But the strongest men were no match for Krishna. One after another Krishna brought them down. He won the contest, and walked up to King Kamsa to receive the prize.

The king, of course, knew well who this young man was; he could see in the handsome features the resemblance to his daughter. There was no doubt that this was the eighth child he had thought dead. But the evil king was certain he could deal with him. Holding the golden cup in his hand, he said: "I have filled the cup with my best wine to refresh you after the hard work of the contest. Come, drink, my friend." But King Kamsa had put a terrible poison into the wine; one drop of it was enough to kill a man. Krishna looked at the cup that was offered to him and said: "You drink from it first, great king." The king trembled, the cup fell from his hands, and he turned and ran to his palace.

Krishna followed, for he knew it was his task to kill Kamsa. When the king saw Krishna coming towards the palace, he sent his guards and soldiers out to fight him. But Krishna struck at them with his sword and they scattered before him, as if he were a mighty army. Then King Kamsa sent out his herd of war-elephants to attack Krishna. However, Krishna pulled out his flute and played it, and the great beasts went down on their knees before him and let him pass.

And so he entered the palace. Everybody had fled except King Kamsa who knew there was no escape, and that the hermit's prophecy would come true. Then Krishna asked him: "What have I done that you tried to poison me?" Kamsa said: "You are the eighth child of my daughter, and it was foretold that you would kill me. So I tried to kill you first, when you were still a baby." And Krishna said: "How was it that I was saved?" Kamsa answered: "I must have killed another child in your place, thinking it was you." With a voice like thunder, Krishna replied: "You have killed a helpless child, and you have offended the gods by the evil you have done." In despair Kamsa drew his sword, but Krishna was ready for him. He struck him down and Kamsa died.

The people of the land rejoiced that the evil king had gone. And now Krishna became king. His real parents came to live with him, and his foster-parents were well rewarded. For many years Krishna ruled his kingdom with wisdom and power. He fought against evil wherever he found it; he helped Arjuna in the great battle against Durodhana. And when Krishna died, his soul joined the gods as one of them.

The Peasant's Reward

In India, there lived a king who was very fond of riding. Every morning he would have one of his fiery horses brought from the stables, and he would go out riding alone for several hours. Now it happened, one day, that the horse he rode was a rather ill-tempered stallion. As they passed a field, a bird suddenly rose up and the horse was so startled by this that it shied and simply ran away. It galloped wildly and the king could do nothing with spurs, or whip, or reins to stop it. At any moment the wild horse could throw him off.

A peasant had been working in the field and when he saw a man on a run-away horse, he left his work and ran across the field. When the horse came near, he snatched at the reins and, being a strong man, pulled the horse to a stop.

The king was badly shaken by this wild ride. He was very grateful to the peasant and he said to him: "My good man, you have saved the life of your king and you shall have a royal reward for it. Come tomorrow to the palace and collect your reward."

The peasant was very pleased to hear that he was going to be given a reward, and he and his wife made great plans how they would use the money he would be given. Early next morning he was at the palace gate.

At the gate a soldier stood guard. "What do you want in the royal palace?" he asked. The peasant explained why he had come. "Well," said the soldier, "you know you cannot get into the palace unless I let you in, and unless I let you in you can't get your reward. And, as I am a poor soldier who

THE PEASANT'S REWARD

can do with some extra money, I will only let you in if you promise me at least some share of your reward."

"Alright," said the peasant, "I don't mind letting you have a few gold pieces." – "Oh no," said the soldier, "I want at least one sixth of whatever you will get." The poor peasant could not help himself and agreed to give the soldier one sixth of his reward.

He went through the gate and into the palace, and then he saw the king's general in a splendid uniform. "What does a peasant want in the palace?" asked the general. Again the peasant explained the business on which he had come. "Well," said the general, "you can't see the king unless you first see the king's secretary who has to ask the king if he is ready to see you. Only I can take you to the secretary. But I will not take you to the secretary unless I get a share of your reward."

"Good heavens," said the peasant, "it seems everyone here wants a share of my reward. How much do you want?"

"One third," said the general. "One third, take it or leave it. If you don't promise me one third, I won't take you to the secretary and you will not see the king or get any reward at all." The peasant could do nothing else but promise he would give the general one third of the reward.

The general took him to the king's secretary and told him why the peasant had come. As soon as the general had left, the secretary said: "My good man, you realise that without me you cannot see the king at all. If I don't go to the king and ask him if it is his royal pleasure to see you, you simply are not allowed to see him. And for doing you this great service, I want one half of your reward."

The peasant thought for a moment. "Alright," he said with a grim smile. "I promise you shall have half of my reward and I hope you will enjoy it."

The secretary went into the great hall where the king was with his courtiers, and told him that a peasant had arrived who expected a reward. "Bring him in," cried the king, "bring him in. This man has saved me from breaking a leg or even from breaking my neck, and no reward is enough for him."

And so at last the peasant stood before the king. "Well, my friend," said the king, "you are most welcome here, and it gives me great pleasure to reward you for a deed that was both kind and brave. Name any reward you like. It is yours!"

"Thank you very much for your kindness," said the peasant, "but I would like the sentry on the gate, your general, and your secretary to be present when I get the reward."

"Certainly," said the king, a bit puzzled. And at his command, the soldier, the general, and the secretary were brought in.

"Now, name your reward," said the king

"Well," said the peasant, "I have a rather peculiar wish."

"Never mind," said the king, "I promise you that whatever it is, if it is at all in my power, you shall have it."

"Thank you, your majesty," said the peasant. "Now what I wish is sixty strokes with a cane."

"Are you mad?" asked the King.

"You promised, your majesty, to give me whatever I wanted," said the peasant. "Surely it is in your power to let me have sixty strokes with a cane."

Well, the king had promised but he was also greatly puzzled. He called for the man whose job it was to punish lazy slaves, and in came a tall negro with a long, stout cane.

"Alright," said the king, "this man here is to be given sixty juicy strokes right away!"

"Just one moment," cried the peasant. "I have promised to share my reward: the soldier gets one sixth, the general gets one third, and the secretary gets one half."

The king laughed aloud when he heard this, and the soldier, the secretary, and the general got their share alright. How much did they get? Was there any left for the peasant?

Then the king sent the peasant home with a bag of gold coins.

The Tiger and the Monkey

There lived once a Brahmin who had spent many years as a hermit in the forest. Although he had no power over animals, he could understand their language. He could speak to animals and they, in turn, could speak to him.

One day the Brahmin walked through a village. It was early morning and the peasants were still asleep. Beside the road was a great iron cage, and inside the cage was a tiger. And the tiger said: "I am dying of thirst. These people caught me yesterday, and they have not given me any water. Oh, good Brahmin, let me out so that I can go to the river and quench my thirst. I promise you when I have had a drink, I will come back to the cage and you can lock me in again."

The Brahmin was very kind-hearted and, as the tiger had promised to come back into the cage, he drew the bolt of the cage door and opened it. The tiger came out, and both the tiger and the Brahmin walked into the forest and down to the river where the tiger quenched her thirst. But then the tiger said: "And now, you foolish man, I am going to kill you and to eat you!"

"What about your promise," cried the Brahmin.

"More fool you, for trusting the promise of a tiger," replied the tiger. "You deserve to die for being so stupid as to believe I would keep my promise."

"Do at least one thing," said the Brahmin. "Let us ask another animal if it is really right that you should kill me."

"I don't mind," said the tiger. "Ask as many animals as you like. They will all say I should eat you."

The first animal they found was a cow. When the cow had heard the story she said: "I don't like human beings. They make me work for them pulling ploughs and they take away the milk which should go to my calf. And besides, if the tiger does not eat the Brahmin he may come and eat me. Go ahead, tiger, and eat the Brahmin."

"Let us try another animal," cried the Brahmin.

"I don't mind," the tiger said.

The next animal they found was an eagle. When the eagle had heard the story he said: "I don't like human beings. They shoot at me with their arrows, and they make a great fuss when I catch one of their lambs. You are right, tiger, go and eat that man."

The Brahmin was in despair; it seemed that all the animals were against him. "Let us try once more," he cried.

"Well," said the tiger, "I am rather hungry, but I will give you one more chance." Just then a monkey came swinging from the branch of a tree, and the Brahmin turned to him and told him the story.

Now the monkey was more friendly to human beings, and this was a very clever monkey. He said: "Well, I can't really say whether the tiger is right or not unless I can see exactly how it all started. Let us go back to the cage. I want to see the cage first." So the Brahmin, the tiger and the monkey went to the great iron cage.

"Hmm," said the monkey, "so this is the cage."

"Yes," said the tiger, "but hurry up, I am hungry."

"Oh," said the monkey. "I cannot make a decision until I know exactly what happened. Show me, tiger, where you were when the Brahmin came?"

"What a waste of time," said the tiger. He jumped into the cage and said: "I was in here, where I stand now."

"Good," said the monkey. "And now you, Brahmin, tell me, was the door of the cage closed and bolted?"

"Yes," said the Brahmin.

"Then close it and bolt it," said the monkey. The Brahmin did so.

"Well," said the monkey, "now I can tell you my decision. The tiger is back where he was. If you, Brahmin, want to open the door again and let him out, then he would be quite right to kill you and eat you."

"I would not dream of it," cried the Brahmin.

"I hope you won't be as silly as that," said the monkey, and ran off into the forest.

And so the tiger was back where he deserved to be; in the cage, and there he stayed.

Myths of
Persia

Ahura Mazda and Ahriman

You remember that in the stories from ancient India, you heard often about holy men or Brahmins. These Indian holy men went away into the forests and lived alone for many years, to devote all their time and effort to prayer. You see, the people of India considered it a holy thing to withdraw from ordinary life. These days we have all kinds of comforts and pleasures in our lives, yet we also have to work for them. But the holy men or hermits, even the noble Sidhartha who became Buddha, lived without comforts and also without work. For the people of India, holiness began with giving up all the things which belong to ordinary life, both pleasure and work.

However, that kind of holiness can only exist in a hot country like India, where there is no cold winter and where you can find all kinds of sweet fruit in the wild jungle. In the soft air of such a country, where even the cool season is warm, it is not so difficult to live in a forest without doing any work. But a holy man from India would not survive very long if he tried to live that kind of life in a much colder country.

But today I want to tell you about Persia, a country which is quite different from India. Now Persia, or Iran as it is known in modern times, is a country where the summer is very hot indeed, nearly as hot as it is in India. But the winter is terribly cold; icy winds sweep down from high mountains, the streams and rivers are frozen and the cold air cuts like a knife. So the seasons in Persia are stark opposites, just as the country itself is also a land of enormous contrasts.

AHURA MAZDA AND AHRIMAN

There are parts of Persia which are dead, empty desert, while other parts have wonderfully rich, fertile soil.

Many thousands of years ago the people of Persia said: "When spring comes, the days get longer, the sun shines brighter and warmer, so the plants bud and blossom. And all this is the work of the God of Light." And they called this god, who sends light and warmth from the sun, Ahura Mazda, which means 'immense shining light.'

And the people said: "Ahura Mazda is also the god of all that is good, wholesome and beautiful. But the icy blast of winter and the long dark nights are the work of the spirit of darkness. This spirit of darkness is called Ahriman and he is also the spirit of evil; of illness and untruth and of all that is dirty and ugly.

They knew that the good god, Ahura Mazda, is forever at war with Ahriman, the Lord of Darkness, and that we human beings also take part in that war. If we are truthful and honest and clean we help Ahura Mazda, but if we lie and are mean and dirty we help Ahriman. So the ancient Persians said: "The cold blast of winter, which makes us shiver, comes from Ahriman. But Ahura Mazda has given us fire to keep us warm. The flames of the fire rise upwards, like the God of Light from whom they come. So will the souls of good, truthful people rise up to Ahura Mazda when they die. But the souls of liars and the unclean will go down to the cold, dark kingdom of Ahriman."

From the beginning of the world Ahriman had always tried to spoil everything that came from Ahura Mazda. When the God of Light created the plants which are good, useful and beautiful, Ahriman made plants which are poisonous. Then Ahura Mazda created a wonderful being, full of wisdom and power, which was the first man, called

Yima. Ahura Mazda also created a great cow which was the first animal. But Ahriman had an answer to that; he brought death, and the first man and the first cow died.

But Ahura Mazda saved the heart of the first man. He planted it in the earth and from the heart grew a man and a woman, and from them come all human beings. And from the body of the great cow, Ahura Mazda made other animals. But whenever Ahura Mazda made a good or beautiful animal, Ahriman made a ferocious or ugly one. Ahura Mazda made birds and at once Ahriman made poisonous snakes. Ahura Mazda made bees and quickly Ahriman made flies and fleas and bugs. Ahura Mazda made butterflies with beautiful wings and Ahriman made spiders. And when Ahura Mazda made sheep, Ahriman made wolves. And so, in the whole of nature you can see the work of both Ahura Mazda and Ahriman.

Hushang Discovers Fire

The God of Light, Ahura Mazda, had made both human beings and the good animals, the sheep, cattle and deer. And Ahriman, the Lord of Darkness, had made the evil animals, the snakes, ferocious wolves and flies, to pester men and beasts.

Now in Persia, many thousands of years ago, the people could only find food by hunting. There were only wild sheep and cattle, and men had to hunt them with spears and arrows made from sharp stones. But one day, one of these men had a dream. In the dream he saw Ahura Mazda take a cow and a calf from a wild herd. Then the god set them apart from the herd by making a fence of sticks around them.

When the man awoke he called his friends and said: "Ahura Mazda has shown me in a dream what to do. We shall drive cows and calves away from the big herd. If we keep them fenced in we don't need to hunt any more. We shall have our own herd as the calves grow up, and we shall also have the milk of cows to drink." So the people used traps and leather ropes to catch cows and young calves. And they caught them and kept them fenced in, as the god had shown in a dream.

This was a great change. As hunters they had thought only of killing animals. But now as herdsmen, although they still had to kill animals for food, they learnt to look after the young ones and to protect the herds against wolves. They also began to love the animals they looked after. In this way they became better human beings, which was what Ahura Mazda wanted.

But Ahriman did not like this at all and he made the wolves attack the herds, killing a sheep here, a calf there. Men had to be on watch day and night, and they began to think it would be easier just to be hunters again. But again one of the men had a dream. In the dream he saw the god Ahura Mazda, who said: "The wolf, the creature of Ahriman, is evil. But evil can be changed into good, and good is always stronger than evil. Therefore make the wolf your friend and helper."

When the man woke up, he wondered how it was possible to change a savage wolf into a friend and helper? Then he thought: "Perhaps we can try with young ones." So he and his friends went in search of a wolf's lair. In a cave they found four little wolf cubs. The men took the cubs home, fed them and looked after them. Soon the little wolves became fond of the men. They grew up and became strong, but they still followed and obeyed the men who cared for them.

When wild wolves came along, the tame wolves fought them and drove them away. While the men slept at night, the tame wolves kept watch and barked when the wild wolves came near. And these tamed wolves of the Persians were the very first dogs. So although Ahriman had made wolves as enemies of men and their cattle and sheep, Ahura Mazda had shown how evil could be turned into something good; into the first dogs who became man's faithful friends and helpers.

Now that men were herdsmen rather than hunters, more and more of them lived together and they decided to choose one man to be their king. His name was Hushang. He was brave and truthful and, therefore, dear to Ahura Mazda. Up to this time the people of ancient Persia had not yet learnt how to master fire. Indeed, they could not make fire so they could not cook. They ate only raw meat and they could not keep warm in the winter.

One day it happened that Hushang and some followers were in the mountains. A huge dark shape approached them and, when it came nearer, they saw it was a horrible monster with glowing red eyes. From its mouth came clouds of smoke which darkened the sun, and the men who were with Hushang ran away in terror. But Hushang himself was a true servant of Ahura Mazda; he would not allow fear, which comes from Ahriman, to have power over him.

As the monster came even nearer, Hushang lifted a rock and threw it. The creature turned and fled. The rock did not hit the monster but it came down on a stone with such force that sparks flew in all directions. The sparks fell on some dry leaves and twigs, which caught fire and burst into flames. When Hushang saw this, he suddenly knew that this was a way to make fire. Ahura Mazda had rewarded his courage by showing him that fire could be made by striking sparks with stones. That night Hushang and his warriors made the first bonfire and rejoiced.

Fire was a great discovery. Ever since then men have used it for both warmth and cooking, and also to make metals soft for moulding into various shapes. In Persia, every year at the time when we have Christmas, there was a great festival in memory of King Hushang, the first man to make fire. And fires, torches and candles were lit at this festival which was called *Shdeh*.

King Djemshid's Golden Dagger

You remember that, at first, the people in ancient Persia were hunters. Hunting was the only way to find the food they needed to eat. Even today there are in some parts of Africa, for instance, people who live only by hunting. These African hunting tribes are, if we compare their way of life with ours, primitive because they have no permanent homes and no cities or villages. The tribes have to move about all the time to follow the wild animals which they hunt. And so it was with the first people in Persia.

But in the story of King Hushang, you heard how the wild hunters became herdsmen. They looked after their cattle and sheep, and tamed wolves to become the very first dogs. They also learned to make fire. And all these things brought about tremendous changes.

And the people of ancient Persia said: "This great change from hunters to herdsmen is really the work of Ahura Mazda. It was Ahura Mazda, the God of Light, who appeared in dreams and showed us what to do." And when the Persians sat round a blazing fire in the cold winter months, they said: "The fire, with its warmth and light, is also a gift from Ahura Mazda, for he is the god of light and warmth in the world. Even in the darkness and the cold of winter, when Ahriman rules outside in the world, the power of Ahura Mazda is with us through the fire." So the Persians regarded fire as something holy; it was the holy flame of Ahura Mazda that kept Ahriman at bay.

But now that people had taken the step from hunters to herdsmen, Ahura Mazda wanted them to make an even greater step; the most important step of all. And there came a time when a king called Djemshid was the ruler of the Persian people. By now people had quite big herds of cattle and sheep, and they had not only tamed dogs but also horses. However they still moved about; when the herds had eaten the grass in one place they had to move to another part of the grasslands. They did not wander about as much as hunters would have done, but neither did they stay for very long in any one place.

One night King Djemshid had a dream. He saw Ahura Mazda holding a golden dagger in his hand. Then the God of Light stabbed the earth with the dagger. From out of the earth grew a stalk and on the stalk there were grains of golden wheat. Then Ahura Mazda gave the dagger to King Djemshid.

When the king woke up, he wondered what the dream meant. The dagger was surely a weapon against Ahriman, but what kind of weapon would make things grow? Then, suddenly, King Djemshid understood what Ahura Mazda had shown him. With his own hands, he went out and made the first plough. Now the plough is really a kind of sword or dagger. Of course, it is not designed to wound human beings, rather it is used to cut through the earth and the soil. Then the king tied a cow to the plough and he ploughed the first furrows. When he had ploughed the field, he picked the grains from a special kind of grass, which we call wheat, and planted them in the furrows.

His people, meanwhile, had been wondering what the king was doing. A year later they saw a field full of golden ears of wheat. King Djemshid showed them how the grains could be made into flour, and how the flour could be used to make bread. Soon they all set about making 'the golden dagger' of Ahura Mazda, or ploughs, out of wood. So they ploughed, sowed grains, and in time, harvested the first crop and made their own bread.

In this way the Persian herdsmen became farmers and peasants. And this was the next great step. For the peasant stays by his field and needs a permanent house. Later on all the other people in the world learned to make ploughs, to till the land, to grow crops and to make bread. But the Persians were the first, and it all began when Ahura Mazda showed King Djemshid a golden dagger in a dream.

Zarathustra and the Kingdom of Light

The Baby who Laughed at Birth
The people of Persia helped Ahura Mazda in his war against Ahriman in two ways. In one way they helped the God of Light by being farmers. Every animal they tamed; dog, cattle, sheep and horse, every furrow they ploughed, every grain they sowed, was a blow against Ahriman. For Ahriman, the Lord of Darkness, wanted to keep the earth and all things on it wild. But they also helped Ahura Mazda by becoming better men, by becoming more civilised. They knew that every lie, every untruth, helps the forces of darkness.

The Persians were quite different from the Indians who thought it was a holy thing to withdraw from work and life and be a hermit. The Persian farmer thought of himself as a warrior against Ahriman. His weapons were truthfulness in himself and, outside in nature, it was the plough or the golden dagger of Djemshid.

But Ahriman fought back. He sent hail storms which destroyed many crops, he sent floods so that herds were drowned, he sent frost in the spring which killed the budding plants, and he sent sand storms from the desert which covered fields and killed crops. Yet the farmers never gave up; when one crop was ruined they patiently planted the next one.

When Ahriman saw that he could not beat the farmers in this way, he tried something else. Both Ahura Mazda and Ahriman had spirits or angels who served them. There were Angels of Light who served Ahura Mazda, and Angels of Darkness who served Ahriman. The Angels of Darkness bring mean thoughts, lies, fear and laziness to human beings. So Ahriman sent out his dark messengers. They could not be seen but, invisibly, they whispered evil advice to human souls. At first just a few, but later more and more people followed the wicked thoughts sent by Ahriman. They became lazy and did not work their fields as well as they could have done, and they began to cheat and lie.

Worse things were to come. Even the priests, who should have served Ahura Mazda, became evil. Through the messengers of Ahriman they learned the use of magic powers. People became afraid of them and did the bidding of the priests out of fear. When Ahura Mazda saw how the evil spread, the god decided that a man would be born in the land of Persia who would become a great leader. This leader would teach people the true and good way of life, and so break the power of Ahriman.

But even before this child was born on earth, Ahriman and his evil helpers got to work. The parents were simple peasants; the father's name was Pourushaspa and the mother was called Daghdu. Ahriman knew the child would fight against him so, when Daghdu was still expecting, the Lord of Darkness sent out an army of evil spirits. They came as a vast black cloud that covered the whole sky, and that cloud was made up of thousands and thousands of horrible creatures; tigers with bats' wings; vultures with tigers' paws and snakes with wolves' heads.

But just before the cloud of monsters pounced on Daghdu, a host of angels appeared carrying swords made of rays of light. These angels of Ahura Mazda struck down the monsters. They screamed and yelled and screeched, then fled in all directions. Again the sun shone clear and bright in the sky, and Daghdu sank down on her knees to praise Ahura Mazda who had saved her.

Ahriman's plan to kill the mother had failed and, in time, Daghdu gave birth to a baby son. Now all babies cry when they are born but this baby was different: he laughed with a clear voice. It was the laughter of a tiny baby, yet the laughter could be heard everywhere on earth. It lasted only a few moments, but in those moments this laughing baby could be heard everywhere. And the laughter itself did something to everyone who heard it.

All good people and good spirits in the world, for instance, felt a great happiness when they heard the baby's laughter. It was as if a great joy had come upon them. But all evil people and evil spirits, all those who were under the spell of Ahriman, felt a sudden fear. They felt terror at the sound of the laughter, and hid themselves in dark corners and holes until the terrible sound stopped.

All over the whole earth the laughter was heard, and it gave joy to all that was good and struck terror in all that was evil. And the parents of the baby who laughed called their little son Golden Star, which in the Persian language is Zarathustra.

Zarathustra Survives the Flames
The little Zarathustra laughed when he came into the world, and the merry sound of his laughter also reached Ahriman. Even the Lord of Evil trembled when he heard laughter that was like the tinkling of silver bells. But when the sound of the child's laughter ceased, there was rage and fury in the ice-cold heart of Ahriman. He, the Lord of

Darkness, the Prince of Black Spirits, the King of Lies, had been shaken by the tiny sounds of a little child. He knew who that baby was, he knew from where this hateful laughter had come, and he swore revenge.

Now the land where Pourushaspa and Daghdu lived was ruled by King Duransarun who was a wicked man. He willingly opened his heart and mind to the black thoughts which came from Ahriman. And the dark spirits whispered: "The new-born child of Pourushaspa and Daghdu is a danger to you and must not be allowed to grow up. It will be much easier to kill him now, rather than wait until he is a grown-up man who will challenge your powers."

The next day King Duransarun set out for the poor little hut of Pourushaspa and Daghdu. When the king arrived, the mother and father were both out in the fields working and had left the baby asleep in a little cot. He opened the door of the hut, walked in and found himself alone with the sleeping child, Zarathustra. The king looked at the baby with a grim smile: never again would the parents hear the child's voice; never would this child grow to manhood and challenge the power of evil in the world.

Swiftly King Duransarun drew a sharp dagger he had brought with him, and lifted his hand to plunge it into the child's breast. But at that moment the baby opened its eyes and looked at the hand that held the dagger. Instantly the king's hand became numb. His whole right arm lost its strength and withered, so that it became like a dry stick. The dagger fell with a clatter to the floor. Speechless with terror, the king looked at his dead arm and hand. Then he turned and fled from the house. He ran like mad to get away from the child whose glance had made his right arm and hand useless for the rest of his life.

Now King Duransarun hated Zarathustra even more than before. He would not go near the baby again but, as he was a king, he could send his servants. So he called two of his men and said: "I command you to take the child of the peasant Pourushaspa and throw it into a fire. Do not come back until you have done the deed, or you will both be burnt alive."

The two men went and hid near the hut until they saw Pourushaspa and Daghdu go out into the fields to work. When they were certain that the parents were so far away that they could not see what was happening, the servants quickly entered, took the baby from its cot and hurried away. Much to their surprise the child made no sound; it did not cry and did not seem to mind.

One of them carried the child while the other man carried a load of dry wood. They walked for a long time until they reached the desert. Then they made a great fire and when it was burning fiercely, they took the child and threw it in. Then they went away laughing; it had been so easy to do the king's bidding. They went back to Duransarun and told him that he need not give another thought to the baby; its life had ended in a great fire in the desert.

In the meantime, the parents of Zarathustra returned from their work and found the cot empty. The poor mother was desperate. She ran out of the house and began to search for her child. Perhaps a wolf had come and dragged it away? Perhaps the baby had fallen from the cot and crawled away? She could not think what had happened, but she would not rest until she had found it.

At long last, when it was getting dark, Daghdu saw a glow of fire out in the desert. With dread and fear in her heart, she rushed towards it. But when she came near she saw a strange sight. The fire had nearly burnt down but in the glowing embers sat Zarathustra, smiling and playing with the little tongues of flames as if they were his toys. And he was quite unharmed. Crying with happiness, Daghdu snatched him up and took him home.

The story of what had happened to the child, how fire would not harm him, spread. People talked about Zarathustra. They said the infant must surely be loved by Ahura Mazda, the Lord of Fire. And when King Duransarun came to hear that Zarathustra was still alive, he began to think of another way to destroy the child.

Flight to a New Land
King Duransarun had failed twice to destroy Zarathustra. But he was all the more determined to bring about the death of the child. He knew the boy could not be killed by weapons because he had lost the use of his right arm when he had tried to stab him. Nor could the child be killed by fire. But there were still other ways. He called the two servants and said: 'The last time you failed to make an end of this child. Do not fail me this time. I want the child thrown to wild beasts. Go and see to it that my will is done."

By now the parents of Zarathustra were afraid to leave the child alone, for strange things had happened. But they were poor peasants, and if they did not both work in the fields there would not be enough to eat. They could only trust that Ahura Mazda, who had protected the child from the flames, would continue to watch over him.

Again the two servants of King Duransarun waited until the child was alone while the parents worked.

And again they took Zarathustra and carried him away. But this time they went into the forest and searched until they found a wolves' den; a cave where wolves lived. As they came near the cave, a large grey wolf's head looked out. The beast snarled and bared its fangs. But they had no wish to fight the savage wolf. Quickly one of them took the baby and threw it into the cave. Then they both ran for their lives. They went back to the king and said: "We have thrown the child to the fiercest wolf in the forest and that, surely, is the end of it."

When Zarathustra's parents came back, once again they found the cot empty. They searched desperately for the child and came, at long last, to the wolves' den in the forest. Inside, Pourushaspa and Daghdu could hear yelping and barking. Fearfully the mother peeped in: there was her child Zarathustra playing with two wolf cubs. He pulled at their tails and they licked his hands with their little red tongues. And two enormous old wolves, the he-wolf and she-wolf, sat there happily, as if the boy were a member of their family.

Daghdu walked in, trembling, expecting any moment to be attacked by the big beasts. But they sat quietly on their haunches. Even when she took the child and walked out, they did not stir. And once more Zarathustra was restored safe and sound to his parents.

Again the news that Zarathustra was unharmed came to King Duransarun. He looked at his withered right hand, which was still not avenged, and his face was grim when he called his two servants. The evil king said: "You have failed again. There is a helpless baby and you two cannot dispose of it! It will go ill with you if this child is not destroyed. As wild beasts have spared it, perhaps tame animals will not be so merciful. Go and see to it that the child is trampled to death by a herd of cattle."

Off the two servants went, and once again they took the child away when the parents were out in the fields working. This time they carried Zarathustra to a narrow lane where, every evening, a large herd of cattle passed by to drink from a nearby river. The bulls and cows were so used to coming this way that no herdsman ever went with them. The men laid the child down in the middle of the lane. Then they went back to King Duransarun and said to him that nothing in the world could save the infant from the hooves of the beasts.

It had been a hot day. The herd of cattle had been out grazing in the burning sun and were very thirsty. They came running down the lane, and the sound of their hooves was like thunder. Galloping in front of the rest was an enormous black bull, the oldest and strongest of the herd. But when that big black bull came to the little bundle, the babe that lay in his path, he stopped. The huge animal took a step forward and stood right over the child, so the other bulls and cows had to squeeze past to the right and the left.

The old bull stood like a rock in a river, and the rest of the herd flowed like waves to either side of him. While the other animals drank at the river, the bull stayed and stood guard over the baby. Eventually the peasants wondered why the bull did not join the herd and when they came to look, they found a baby lying safe and sound between the animal's four legs. Only when the child was taken away did the old bull go down to the river to drink.

By now, Zarathustra's parents realised that it was King Duransarun who had tried again and again to kill their child. So they decided to flee. Secretly one night they left their home and travelled out of the country where Duransarun, the servant of Ahriman, held power. Eventually they came to another part of Persia where King Vishtaspa ruled. This king was not evil and neither did he know anything of the child Zarathustra, beloved of Ahura Mazda, that had come into the world.

The Angel Good Thought

The parents of Zarathustra had fled with their child to a part of Persia ruled by King Vishtaspa. In that part of the country people knew nothing of Ahura Mazda. Although King Vishtaspa was not an evil man, his advisers were priests who used black magic. These cunning men worshipped the demons sent by Ahriman, and often they could make the king do what they wanted. And in this part of Persia, where people knew nothing of Ahura Mazda and evil priests advised the king, Zarathustra grew up.

Even as a young man, he was different from others of his age. He liked to be alone; he went for long walks by himself and thought much about the evil around him. He felt great sorrow and wondered what could be done to change things. One day, when he was deeply in thought about these matters, he came to the banks of a river; Zarathustra had been walking for quite a long time, he had wandered far away, and there were no other people for miles and miles.

As he stood by the river, it seemed very quiet around him; no wind stirred the grass; no leaves rustled in the trees. As he wondered about the strange silence, suddenly there stood before him a large figure, dazzling white and nine times as tall as a human being. In one hand this figure of light held a long staff that shone like gold.

Then the figure spoke to him and said: "I am the messenger from the God of Light, Ahura Mazda, and my name is Good Thought (or Vohuman, in Persian). From my master I have brought every good and true thought that has ever appeared in human minds. And I have come to take you with me to Ahura Mazda, for you shall see the Lord of Light face to face. But only your spirit can rise up to the heavens where Ahura Mazda rules, not your body. Your body must remain here on earth."

After the angel spoke these words, it seemed to Zarathustra that his body was like a coat or a garment which he could take off. He left his body lying on the ground, his spirit soared upwards together with the angel Good Thought, and they entered the kingdom of pure light, the kingdom of Ahura Mazda. In this Kingdom of Light nothing throws any shadow and all things and all beings shine with light, the light of goodness that comes from themselves. Here on earth goodness does not show itself so easily, but in the Kingdom of Light goodness actually shines.

And there, in the Kingdom of Light, where there is no shadow and goodness shines, Zarathustra saw hosts upon hosts of angels and archangels. (The angels are higher than man, just as archangels are higher than angels.) Then he saw Ahura Mazda himself, the lord of angels and archangels. The god spoke to Zarathustra and gave him rules of good thoughts, good words and good deeds. And Zarathustra knew that he had to teach these rules to men on earth.

Then the angel Good Thought brought him back to his body which lay on the ground as if it were dead. Zarathustra put on the body, as one puts on a coat, and set out to teach men the way of life that would lead them to the Kingdom of Light.

Before long, Ahriman saw that people turned away from evil and he was losing power over them. When they died they no longer came to his domain of pitch black darkness and everlasting cold. They went instead to the Kingdom of Light. So the Prince of Darkness summoned all his monsters and evil spirits and led them to attack and destroy Zarathustra. From the north they came, bringing with them a coldness so terrible that birds fell dead from the air and the earth froze as hard as rock. But Zarathustra spoke the words of a holy prayer which he had learned from Ahura Mazda and the evil spirits lost their power. The air became warm, the ice melted and Ahriman fled.

When Ahriman saw that he could not overcome Zarathustra by force, he tried to destroy him by cunning. He appeared before Zarathustra in the shape of a beautiful angel and said: "Worship me, O Zarathustra. Do what I command you to do, for I am the holiest of the holy angels of light." But Zarathustra said: "I have seen the angels who serve Ahura Mazda. I know that they are not only beautiful when you see their face; they are also beautiful from behind. Turn round and show me your back!"

But Ahriman answered: "Don't make me turn round. I belong to the angels which are different; we are beautiful from the front, but our backs are ugly." Zarathustra replied: "I command you to turn round." The angel who seemed so beautiful turned, and his whole back was nothing but writhing black snakes. Again Zarathustra spoke the holy prayer he had learned from Ahura Mazda and the horrible creature, who was beautiful in front and twisting black snakes from behind, fled in terror. Then Zarathustra set off to see King Vishtaspa to make him a servant of Ahura Mazda.

At the Court of King Vishtaspa

Having driven Ahriman to flight, Zarathustra continued with the task Ahura Mazda had given him. He taught people to have good thoughts, to speak good words and do good deeds, so that at the end of their life they would rise up to the Kingdom of Light.

But he found that many people in that part of Persia would not listen to him. They said: "If what you tell us is true, why is it that our own king does not follow your teaching? Neither our king, his queen, nor his ministers or generals seem to take much notice of you. We are poor, ignorant people, we cannot tell whether we should believe you or not. But if you can persuade the king to worship Ahura Mazda then we, too, will follow and obey the God of Light."

Zarathustra saw that he would make little headway among these people unless he first brought the king to worship Ahura Mazda. But this was not an easy thing for King Vishtaspa had wicked councillors and priests as his advisers. The king was so used to following their advice that it would be very hard to make him change his mind. But Zarathustra, the faithful servant of the God of Light, would not shrink from a task because it was difficult. He prayed to Ahura Mazda to give him help and then set out for the royal court.

Now the king had come to hear of the strange preacher who went through the country telling people of the Kingdom of Light. The wicked priests, however, had told Vishtaspa that the preacher was a magician of the worst kind. They said that Zarathustra used the dead bodies of cats and bats, and the hair of dead dogs to make a horrible witches' brew, and this brew gave him power to send sickness to people. Yet the king had also heard that Zarathustra was gentle and wise, so he was curious to really see what kind of person he was.

King Vishtaspa was seated on his throne. Around him stood his generals in glittering armour and his advisers, the priests in their scarlet robes. A servant entered, prostrated himself before the king (laid himself flat on the ground) and announced that Zarathustra was outside and had asked for permission to see him. At the king's command the slave rose, went out and came back with Zarathustra.

King Vishtaspa and his court saw a tall man with long, black hair and a beard, wearing a long white robe. But what was he carrying in his hand? Was it a candle? Was it a burning torch? As Zarathustra came closer they saw that he carried, in his outstretched hand, a flame of fire. It seemed to grow from the palm of his hand like a flower. It was a flower of fire but his hand was not harmed at all. Then Zarathustra said: "The flame you see in my hand is the sign and proof that I have been sent by the Lord of Light and Fire, by Ahura Mazda. Will you listen to his message?"

King Vishtaspa was astounded. He asked Zarathustra to put out the great flame in his hand, and told him he was willing to listen. Zarathustra spoke to the flame. It went out, and he began to tell Vishtaspa about the Kingdom of Light and the rules of Ahura Mazda. But the evil priests spoke against him and the king did not know who to believe. At the end of the day, Zarathustra was given a house in the palace grounds to rest because the king wanted to talk to him again the next day. But the wicked priests took a dead cat and a dead bat, and hid them in Zarathustra's house when he was away. Then they called the king, showed him the horrible things and said: "We told you he used black magic. Here is the proof." When King Vishtaspa saw this he was furious. The preacher had deceived him and, at his command, Zarathustra was taken and thrown into prison.

Now it happened that King Vishtaspa had a favourite horse, a black stallion. It had carried him through many a battle, and he loved that horse like a friend. But, on the very day that Zarathustra was thrown into prison, his beautiful black horse was struck by a strange illness. The horse lay down and drew up its four legs, which became as stiff as wood. Of course the king was terribly upset. He called doctors and he called the wicked priests, but none of them could help. The horse remained sick.

From his prison cell Zarathustra heard the soldiers who stood on guard talk about the sick horse and Vishtaspa's sorrow. So he called out to the soldiers: "Go to the king and tell him I can cure his horse, but only if he agrees to four conditions." When the king received Zarathustra's message he was overjoyed. On his orders, Zarathustra was released from the prison and brought before him.

They went to the stables where the horse was kept and Zarathustra said: "Will you promise to drive the wicked priests away from your court?" The king said: "I promise," and, in that moment, the horse stretched out one leg. Then Zarathustra said: "Promise to worship Ahura Mazda and to follow the rules of the Kingdom of Light." – "I promise," said the king. Immediately the horse stretched out another leg. Then Zarathustra asked: "Promise that your wife, the queen, will worship Ahura Mazda." Again the king promised, and the horse stretched out a third leg. And Zarathustra said: "I want one more promise. Will your generals and warriors fight for the religion of Ahura Mazda?" After the king gave this last promise, the black stallion stretched out the fourth leg and leapt up.

And King Vishtaspa kept his four promises. The wicked priests were driven out, and the king and queen worshipped Ahura Mazda and lived by the rules of the Kingdom of Light. Once King Vishtaspa and his wife had done so, the people he ruled followed. And his generals and soldiers also swore to defend the religion of Ahura Mazda. But, having kept his promise, King Vishtaspa asked a favour of Zarathustra. Next time you will hear what that favour was.

The Kingdom of Light
King Vishtaspa had kept his promises and he and all his people worshipped Ahura Mazda. But he wanted to be sure that, at the end of his days, he would ascend to the Kingdom of Light. So he said to Zarathustra: "I ask you one favour. Show me at least a glimpse of the Kingdom of Light." Zarathustra raised his arms and prayed that the king's wish should be granted. There was a loud clap of thunder, the earth trembled, and there, in the royal palace, stood three figures of radiant light; three archangels.

The king and his courtiers trembled with fear before these mighty, shining beings. But the archangels spoke to them and calmed their fears. One of them held a golden cup to the lips of King Vishtaspa and said: "Drink from this cup. It contains the Water of Life, and he who drinks the Water of Life can see into the future." So the king drank and in that moment the royal court, his ministers and the angels all seemed to disappear. Then a picture of all that was going to happen to him in years to come spread before his eyes.

King Vishtaspa saw himself leading his armies into battle and his enemies being defeated. And, with every victory, he saw how the religion of Ahura Mazda spread further and further. Then he saw himself as an old man at the end of his life on earth. But this was not all that he saw.

In that great vision, earth was left behind. King Vishtaspa seemed to rise upwards and a bridge woven from rays of the sun appeared before him. For good honest, truthful people the bridge was wide. They could walk safely over it and enter the Kingdom of Light at the other end. But for evil people, for liars and cheats, for the cruel and heartless, the bridge shrank until it was as narrow as the edge of a knife. And they fell down into a dark abyss below, which was the Kingdom of Ahriman.

But King Vishtaspa saw himself walking safely across the bridge and, at the other end, he was welcomed into the Kingdom of Light by the same three archangels who had appeared to him at his palace. So he saw himself enter the world where there is no shadow. Then the vision disappeared and King Vishtaspa was back in his royal court with his ministers, courtiers, Zarathustra and the three shining archangels. And this great picture in which he had seen his future life; the years of battles and victories, his death and what came after, all this had only taken one instant.

The king's wish had been fulfilled, yet the three archangels did more. One of them held a flower before the Grand Vizier, King Vishtaspa's highest minister. As he inhaled the sweet scent of the flower, the Grand Vizier's mind became filled with the highest wisdom so that his advice to the king would always be right. And to the king's highest general they gave a fruit to eat. When he had eaten it he became invulnerable and no weapon could do him any harm.

When they had done this the three archangels blessed King Vishtaspa in the name of Ahura Mazda, and then they disappeared. And the king, his court and all his people looked up with great reverence to the holy man, Zarathustra, who could call the archangels from heaven.

The Golden Star of the Future

All that King Vishtaspa had seen in his vision came to pass. He led his armies into battle and won each time. Vishtaspa's chief adviser was wise above all men, his general could not be wounded by any weapon. No enemy could hope to win against such a king, such a minister and such a general.

In time Vishtaspa became ruler of a great empire where all the people worshipped Ahura Mazda. Many temples were built to the God of Light and the holy fire was kept burning day and night. But where there are temples, there must be priests. Zarathustra was the highest priest of Ahura Mazda, but he needed other priests to help teach the religion of Ahura Mazda, to guard the holy fire in all the temples, and to see that people lived truly by the rules of good thoughts, words and deeds. For this, many priests were needed and Zarathustra chose them from among the best men in Persia. They became his pupils and he taught them what he had seen and heard in the Kingdom of Light. And these pupils of Zarathustra were called Magi.

Many years passed and Zarathustra grew old. When he was an old man, he called the best of the Magi to him and said: "All I have done in my life was only a preparation for something great and wonderful that will happen in the future; in three thousand years time. Then the true saviour of mankind, or *Sayosant*, will be born on earth and he will overcome even death itself. Remember that my name, Zarathustra, means Golden Star. When that true saviour of mankind is born on earth, a golden star will appear in the sky. By the light of this star, my spirit will guide the true and faithful Magi of that time to the place where the holy child is born."

When Zarathustra told this to his pupils he was seventy seven years old and he knew that his own life was coming to an end. But he was not to die peacefully. The evil priests, the servants of Ahriman, had not forgotten that he had driven them from the court of King Vishtaspa, and they wanted revenge. They waited for a time when the old man was by himself, then they fell upon him and murdered him. But they could only kill him because it was time for Zarathustra to leave earth and return to the Kingdom of Light.

Later on King Vishtaspa, the mighty ruler, also died and crossed the great bridge to the Kingdom of Light. After him came other rulers but they were not as good as he was. Slowly, over hundreds of years, the kings of Persia let Ahriman gain power over their hearts and minds. They became evil and cruel, and even among the Magi only a few remained pure, good and wise. The others became magicians, and the word magician actually comes from the word Magi.

And in the fullness of time, after three thousand years, the Jesus child was born in Bethlehem and a radiant golden star shone in the sky. When that star appeared in the heavens there were only three Magi left who knew and understood what this meant. In some books they are called three wise men or three holy kings. They were the last true and faithful Magi or priests of Ahura Mazda, and they travelled from Persia to Bethlehem and brought gifts to the Jesus child. But it was the golden star of Zarathustra which guided them to Bethlehem.

Myths of Babylonia

The Land of Two Rivers

Remember Atlantis, the land of mist and fog. In Atlantis men did not have to work the soil. Instead they used magic powers to make things grow where and when they wanted them. But when Atlantis was swallowed by the ocean, the people who escaped had to make a new start without magic. Yet, as you have seen from the stories, there were always a few people who still knew something about the old magic powers. Some were holy men, and others were wicked men who used black magic for evil purposes. But the ordinary people had to learn to live without magic.

Then you heard how the people of India were always longing for the old times when men did not have to work. Even the gentle Prince Sidhartha who became Buddha left his father's palace to become a hermit and a beggar rather than a peasant. These people of ancient India could never have become the first peasants and farmers. They did, of course, farm, but they learnt about farming later on from the Persians. The art of ploughing, sowing, reaping and the taming of wild animals came to India. But it could never have started in India because the Indian people were never quite at home on the earth.

The Persians were quite different. They wanted to make the earth their home. They changed wild plants and tamed wild animals so that they became useful to man. By doing this they helped Ahura Mazda, the God of Light, in his war against Ahriman. Every ploughed field, every well-tended garden, every tamed animal was a blow against the Lord of Darkness. And with farming came the building of

THE LAND OF TWO RIVERS

villages and towns, and the beginning of civilisation as we know it.

People who are forever on the move are called nomads and a nomad is not really at home anywhere. But when people settle in one place, in villages or towns, they have a home. They are at home in their village, town or city on the earth. But even in Persia people did not live in cities. As peasants and farmers they lived in wooden huts clustered in little villages. The first cities were built in another land altogether, a land where great things were done to make the earth even more of a home for mankind.

This land lies west of Persia and two great rivers called the Euphrates and the Tigris flow through it. Both rivers spring from a mighty, snow-capped mountain range and as they rush down the mountain slopes, a lot of earth is gathered up and carried by the water. But when the Tigris and Euphrates reach the plains, they flow much more slowly and the earth is dropped or deposited. Over thousands of years the land between the rivers has become covered with layers and layers of rich fertile soil. Now you see, once the art of farming had been invented, you could not wish for better farming land than this Land of Two Rivers, which in the Greek language is Mesopotamia.

It was in Mesopotamia that the first great cities in the history of mankind were built. Everywhere else in the world at that time people were still hunting wild animals in the forests, or were just beginning to live in tiny villages. But in Mesopotamia many mighty cities with great temples and soaring towers were being built. And one of them became the largest, mightiest, most beautiful city of them all. It was called Babylon, and it was built on the banks of the Euphrates. And there was a time when the people who built

Babylon, the Babylonians, held sway and ruled the whole Land of Two Rivers, so that it was for a time called Babylonia.

Now there is a reason why the first great cities in the history of the world came to be built in Mesopotamia; cities with names that sound like magic spells: Ur, Niniveh, Ersk, Sippar and, the greatest of them all, Babylon. And this is the story the Babylonians told of how they came to build the first cities in the world.

They said: The light of the sun is not only just light, just something you see with your eyes. The light of the sun is a garment, and in this garment is the God of Wisdom, whose name is Ea. Just as we human beings wear clothes, so Ea wears the light of the sun, the rays of the sun, as his garment. And the time when Ea is strongest and his power wakens all beings is the early morning. In the glowing light of the dawn is Ea, the God of Wisdom.

"And," so said the Babylonians, "our forefathers who lived on the sea-shore saw Ea, the wise spirit of the dawn, rise every morning from the sea and worshipped him. And Ea spoke to our forefathers and said: 'Good and rich and fertile is the soil which the rivers have brought down from the mountains. Wheat and barley for your bread, and lush grain for your herds of cattle and sheep grow from it. But even more can be done with this soil. If you take a lump of this good earth when it is still damp, wet it with river water and knead it in your hands, it will take any shape you want.'

"And Ea said: 'If you mould the clay into an oblong shape and let it dry in the sun, it will become as hard as rock. If you make hundreds of these stones of regular shape you can build houses and wells more lasting than wood.'

And so it was that our forefathers learned from Ea, the wise God of the Dawn, to make bricks."

And that was one of the great inventions made by the people of Babylonia or the Land of Two Rivers. They learnt from Ea to make bricks, and with these bricks they built the first great cities.

Marduk, the God Who Knew No Fear

Let us think of how long ago it was when the people of Mesopotamia learnt to make bricks. The time of King Arthur and his knights was a thousand years ago. Take twice as long, 2000 years ago, and that was the time when Christ lived on earth. And now take not 2000, but 4000 years before Christ and you come to the time when the Babylonians were building their mighty cities. In Europe, however, people were still living very primitively; perhaps in caves, hunting wild boar and deer in the dense forests. But, faraway, in the Land of Two Rivers there were already the great cities of Ur, Niniveh and Babylon.

The walls surrounding Babylon were so thick that a chariot could be driven along the top. In the city itself there were wide avenues and great buildings with splendid decorations. The people of Babylon loved colour and they had learnt to decorate the outside of their buildings with coloured enamelled bricks. They had also discovered that the clay from which the bricks were made could be used for other things. Jars, pots, pans, plates and cups were fashioned out of clay and so pottery came into being.

Now, if you had walked along a street in the city of Babylon, you would have seen people who had dark hair and brown skins. The men grew their hair and beards as long as possible. Their hair was curled and frizzy and oiled to make it look glossy. The men also wore very high hats, long cloaks right down to their ankles, and a long shawl which covered the left arm. The other end was fastened under the right arm, leaving it free. Women had the same kind of dress, but they also wore a head-cloth to cover their faces because it was considered unseemly for a woman to show her face out in the street.

And you would have looked with wonder and admiration at the soaring towers of the city of Babylon. They were a strange shape, and not at all like towers in our time. They looked like boxes put on top of each other; the biggest box was at the bottom, a smaller one sat on top of it, and a still smaller box was above that, until there were seven boxes with the smallest one on top. These mighty towers were temples to the gods of Babylon. And if you had asked a man of Babylon why they built their temples so high, he would have told you the story of the brave god Marduk and the dragon Tiamat.

Once, at the very beginning of all things in the world, there was no rule, no order and no rhythm. There was only disorder, which was a mixture of air, water, fire and earth. There was only chaos and the Lord of Chaos was a dragon called Tiamat. The dragon Tiamat loved chaos and disorder, and he wanted the world to stay untidy and wild without any shape, form or order.

But there were also the good gods and they began to sing. The harmony between their different voices was so wonderful that the whole world rang with it. And the harmonious song of the gods began to bring order into being. The right shapes and forms, and rhythm and beauty appeared in the world. But the mighty dragon Tiamat hated what the gods created with their singing. He destroyed what they had brought into being and swore he would also destroy the gods themselves to make an end of their music. And so powerful was the dragon Tiamat that the gods trembled with fear. Even the gods did not have magic powers as great as the dragon's.

One of these good gods was the wise Ea, God of the Dawn. Yet even he was not strong enough to fight the dragon. But Ea had a son, the young god Marduk. When the gods came together and spoke of their fear that Tiamat would destroy them, Marduk stepped forward and said: "I will fight the dragon and make an end of him." And to show the other gods that he also possessed magic powers, the young Marduk took his cloak from his shoulders and commanded it to disappear. Then he gave another command and the cloak reappeared again. And Ea, his father, and the other gods praised him as the bravest and strongest of them all.

Marduk made a great net, and armed himself with bow and arrows and a mighty club. Then he spoke the words of a magic spell and, at his command, a howling storm carried him through the air to the lair of the dragon Tiamat. The dragon crouched outside his cave. His scaly body gleamed and flames flickered from his eyes and nostrils. When he saw a huge storm approaching carrying the young god Marduk, Tiamat roared terrible magic spells. And these spells would have destroyed anyone who had even the faintest feeling of fear.

But Marduk had no fear at all. His courage was like a great shield, and Tiamat's evil spells could not break through the strength of his courage. Quickly Marduk threw his great net over the dragon. As the monster snarled and opened his huge jaws to tear the net to shreds, Marduk commanded the wind to fly into Tiamat's mouth. It blew in through Tiamat's mouth and down into his body. While the dragon twisted and turned with pain, Marduk lifted his mighty club and shattered the monster's head.

And tomorrow you will hear what this battle between the god Marduk and Tiamat, the dragon, had to do with the high towers of Babylon.

Gilgamesh and Eabani

The Son of the Sun God
When Marduk had killed the dragon Tiamat, he divided the body into two parts. Out of one part he fashioned the blue vault of the sky, and from the other he made the firm earth. All the other gods rejoiced and began to sing again.

But the songs of the gods are much more powerful than human singing. They have magic powers and as the choir of gods sang out in harmony, the stars, the moon and the sun appeared in the sky. Once again there was order, harmony and rhythm in the world. Day and night came into being. There was spring, summer, autumn and winter. The regular rising and setting of the sun, the full moon and the new moon, and the bright stars in the sky at night are all a picture of the music of the choir of gods that sang them into existence.

And the Babylonians said: "You see, nature itself obeys the stars, the sun and the moon. The crops we grow in our fields must be planted at a certain time or they will never ripen. The sheep have their lambs, and the birds build nests and lay their eggs only at a certain time of the year. All creatures obey the great order of sun and moon and stars. And because we people of Babylon also want to live in harmony with the order and rhythm of the heavenly lights, we built the great towers from which our priests observe the stars.

"But our priests not only tell us when to plant our crops. When a child is born, they can tell from the stars if that child will make a good merchant or warrior or peasant, and whether he will be strong or weak, bright or dull. Our king would not go to war unless the priests had told him the stars were in his favour. Nor would a merchant go on a business journey, a doctor perform an operation or a captain sail his ship unless the priests, who understand the music of the stars, say the heavenly lights are favourable."

So now you know that these mighty towers, three hundred feet high, were used for observing and studying the stars. The priests of Babylon were the first astronomers and the first people who began to measure time. They knew that the year has three hundred and sixty five days which could be divided into twelve months. They worked out a week of seven days and they knew that between one full moon and another twenty eight days or four weeks passed. The priests also divided the day into twenty four hours, every hour into sixty minutes and every minute into sixty seconds.

But they did not have the sort of watches and clocks that we use today. The Babylonians invented simple ways of telling the time such as the sun clock which showed the hour by the shadow thrown by a stick. They also used water clocks. These were bowls with a little hole through which water fell, drop by drop into a lower pot. After one hour the upper pot was empty. And they had sand clocks where, in exactly one hour, the sand ran from an upper vessel into a lower one.

So our modern watches and the division of time into years, months, weeks, hours, minutes and seconds all goes back to the priests in ancient Babylon six thousand years ago. It all came from watching the sun, the moon and the stars so that here on earth there should be the same order as in the heavens.

You have heard how the priests watched the stars, and when a child was born they could tell its future. Usually the parents listened to the advice of the priests and planned the child's life so that it would be in harmony with the stars. But sometimes people ignored the advice of the priests. And the Babylonians told a story about a king who tried to oppose the stars, who tried to prevent something which the priests said would happen.

The king was the ruler of the city of Erek. One day the priests told him that his daughter would have a child. But they also said that this child would, in time, take both the kingdom and the king's life. But the king was a cruel man and he decided that there was one easy way to prevent all this. If his daughter never married, she would not have a child and his throne would be safe. So he commanded that the poor princess be locked up in a prison at the top of a high tower.

For a long time the princess was left alone in her prison. But a day came when the Sun God looked down from his throne in the sky and saw the beautiful maiden through a window in the tower. He fell in love with the princess and, as the sunlight shone into her prison, the Sun God changed into the shape of a handsome young man. He became her husband, but after six months the Sun God had to return to his golden throne in the sky. The princess was alone again, but she was not sad because she was expecting a baby. And, in time, a child was born to her. The princess was very happy and called her son Gilgamesh.

But the king of Erek began to wonder how his daughter was getting on. He climbed the stairs up to the prison on top of the tower, unlocked the door with his key and walked in. When he saw his daughter holding a child, his face grew red with fury and hatred. He snatched the child from her arms and threw it out of the window.

However, at that moment, a great eagle swooped down from the sky, caught the child in mid-air and flew away with him. And a great fear came over the king of Erek for now he knew that the prophecy of the priests would come true.

Gilgamesh Finds a Friend
The eagle who had rescued the child flew far from the city of Erek. At last the great bird landed in a garden, put the baby gently down and then flew away. The peasant who owned the garden found the little boy and, as he and his wife had no children, they were very happy and looked after the child as if it was their own.

But the couple soon learned who the boy was. The king of Erek sent his soldiers out to find the child he had thrown out of the window. They searched the countryside and asked everyone if they had seen the princess's baby. The peasant and his wife pretended the child was their own so the little boy was safe.

When Gilgamesh was old enough, his foster-parents told him that he was not their son but of royal blood. And when they told him how his cruel father kept his mother imprisoned in a tower, the young Gilgamesh swore that, one day, he would set her free. He was tall and strong, stronger than any other man, and people could feel when they met him that he was more than an ordinary human being. He was the son of the Sun God and he had a certain power and majesty which made people look up to him. So when he called his peasant friends together and told them he was going to fight the king of Erek, they willingly took up arms and followed him in their thousands.

Gilgamesh led his army to the city of Erek. They surrounded the city and laid siege to it. For three years the city of Erek held out as the king and his soldiers fought against Gilgamesh's army. But in the end there was no food left. The soldiers grew weak and, in the streets of Erek, men and women cried with hunger. Then Gilgamesh and his men broke through the gates of the city walls and stormed in. The evil king was killed by an arrow from Gilgamesh's bow, and his soldiers laid down their arms and hailed Gilgamesh as the new king of Erek. With great joy, Gilgamesh climbed the steps of the tower up to his mother's prison and set her free. And in this way the prophecy of the priests, all that they had read in the stars, had come to pass.

But Gilgamesh was not a good king for the city of Erek. He wanted to be famous as a great builder. He wanted to raise walls and towers so mighty that for hundreds of years people should look up at them with awe and say: "This was built by the great Gilgamesh."

He even ordered all the able-bodied men of Erek to leave their work. Instead they had to make bricks and build great new walls and soaring towers. Overseers with whips walked among the men and lashed out mercilessly if they showed any signs of slacking. Great was the sorrow and unhappiness in Erek under the harsh rule of Gilgamesh and the people prayed to the gods for help.

One day a man who had come from the mountains began to live outside the city walls. Such a man no one had seen before; he was of enormous height, his body was covered with hair like an animal and his beard stretched down to his waist. But strangely, the animals came to this wild man without fear. Birds flew to his hand if he called them, lions came to him like dogs and obeyed him, and even the wild deer laid down beside him. And for a time this wild man, who was called Eabani, roamed the countryside outside the city of Erek.

Gilgamesh, the king, had never met anyone who was his equal in strength and when he heard about the enormous Eabani, he wanted to meet him. With great curiosity he set off through the city gates and found the wild man. He challenged him and said: "Let us see who is stronger. If you win you can be king of Erek." Eabani accepted the challenge and the two tall, strong men began to wrestle. They strained every muscle. They heaved and pulled with all their strength, and for a whole day and a whole night they struggled against each other.

When morning came they were both exhausted and they knew that neither of them could win. Then Gilgamesh said: "Now I have found a man who is as strong as I am. Be my friend, Eabani, and share with me the power I have as king of Erek." From that day on Gilgamesh and Eabani became like brothers. They ruled the city of Erek together. And Eabani, who looked wild but was so gentle that animals came to him as friends, changed many things. Through Eabani, Gilgamesh too became gentle and kind, and he ceased to make the people of Erek work like slaves.

Now in the land which Gilgamesh and Eabani ruled there was a great forest where a terrible monster called Khumbaba lived. No one ever went into the forest for fear of meeting the monster which had the head of a crocodile, the body of a great serpent, claws like a lion and breath that was like burning fire. But the two friends decided that if they went together they would be strong enough to conquer Khumbaba. So Gilgamesh and Eabani set out for the great gloomy forest, where no birds sang and no animals could be heard or seen. Then they saw a cave out of which came a long snout. Above the snout two red eyes glowered at them. The next moment the whole huge monster appeared and came rushing towards them with open jaws.

As the monster lifted its paw to knock down Gilgamesh, Eabani dealt it a terrible blow on the back with his club. Khumbaba gave a horrible scream and turned on Eabani, but Gilgamesh hit it hard on the head with his club. Wild with fury, Khumbaba turned to attack Gilgamesh. Now Eabani struck again and the blow broke its spine. As Khumbaba's jaws snapped savagely at Eabani, he quickly leapt aside and Gilgamesh brought his club down with such shattering force that it crushed the monster's head. And so the two friends had done together what a single man could not have done alone; they had slain the monster Khumbaba.

The Curse of the Goddess Ishtar
The story of Gilgamesh and Eabani you have been hearing is perhaps the very first story that was ever written down in the history of mankind. But it was not written down on parchment or paper or in a book. The ancient Babylonians did not have books or paper for they had not yet been invented. So let us see how the first writing came about.

You remember how Ea, the God of Wisdom, had taught people to use the earth which the rivers Euphrates and Tigris brought down from the mountains. Out of this clay the Babylonians made bricks for their buildings. But there was something else which Ea taught them. He showed them how to make oblong slabs from the clay which were called tablets. Then he taught people how to scratch signs, which were the first letters, on these tablets.

Of course, the letters were not at all like the letters of the alphabet we use when we write. And we use pens and ink, while the Babylonians only had a little stick with square ends to write with. When each tablet was filled with writing it was treated in the same way as a brick. It was dried in the sun, or baked in an oven, and became as hard as stone.

So a book in ancient Babylonia was a collection of inscribed bricks or tablets. If you had a library of many books you really had stacks and stacks of hard baked tablets or bricks.

Nowadays a book made of inscribed clay tablets would seem very clumsy, but such a book lasts much longer than our flimsy paper books. And that is why, after more than 5000 years, some Babylonian writing still exists.

Today we know the story of Gilgamesh and Eabani only because it was written in wedge-shaped letters and preserved on hard baked tablets. And it took many very clever people years of hard work to discover how to read this ancient writing. The proper name for it is cuneiform writing, and in the British Museum, in London, there are hundreds of these tablets inscribed with the stories and myths of ancient Babylon.

The story of Gilgamesh and Eabani, as it is written on the hard tablets, goes like this: When the two friends had slain the monster Khumbaba, they returned in triumph to the city of Erek. A great celebration was held. Gilgamesh dressed himself in royal robes and all the people hailed him and Eabani for their great deed.

Now among the gods of Babylon was a goddess whose name was Ishtar. She was the Goddess of Beauty and Love and she often fell in love with handsome young men. She would take human shape and appear to the man she loved as a beautiful woman. But after a short time, Ishtar always got tired and left him for another good-looking young man.

When Ishtar saw Gilgamesh in his regal splendour she fell in love with him. As soon as the celebration was over she changed into a woman more beautiful than any mortal woman could ever be, and said to him: "Be my bridegroom, Gilgamesh, and I will give you victory in all your wars. I will make your herds of cattle increase a hundredfold, and you will be rich and powerful above all men."

But Gilgamesh knew that Ishtar was a fickle goddess who would never be faithful to any man. And he said: "I know of the men you have loved before and you have deserted them all. I do not want to have anything to do with you." Ishtar pleaded with him but he scorned her. In the end Gilgamesh became quite rude and told her she was shameless and that nothing in the world would make him follow her. Never before had Ishtar been scorned by a man. Boiling with rage she left Gilgamesh, thirsting for revenge.

There was one thing though that Ishtar had to consider. Gilgamesh was the son of the Sun God and so she could not deal with him as she might have liked. But she could hurt him in other ways; she could make the people of the city of Erek suffer. And this she did by sending an enormous black bull down from the mountains. It trampled the fields and ruined the crops. The peasants were terrified and fled from their work.

When Gilgamesh heard about the wild bull he went out to the fields where it was rampaging. The bull lowered its horns and rushed towards Gilgamesh to gore him. At the last moment he jumped aside and plunged his sword into the bull's neck and the great beast fell down dead. Eabani had also come to help, and now the two friends tied ropes to the bull's horns and began to drag the carcass back towards the city. As they came near Erek, they saw Ishtar standing up on the wall surrounding the city. The goddess was very angry that the bull had been killed and she cursed

Gilgamesh loudly. But her curses had no power over the son of the Sun God and Gilgamesh laughed at her.

But Eabani did not like to hear his friend cursed. He cut a piece off the dead bull with his sword, threw it down and shouted at Ishtar: "That's what I will do to you if you don't keep quiet!" The Goddess of Beauty looked down at him from the wall and spoke a mighty spell which carried the curse of death. Then she disappeared.

In that hour Eabani fell ill. All the doctors and priests of Erek could not heal him and after twelve days he died. Gilgamesh was heart-broken over the loss of his friend and the thought came to him that he would also die one day. He wondered if there was a way out; if any human being could escape death and live on earth for ever. He went to ask the priests, and from them he learnt there was a man who knew the secret of life without death.

The Plant of Life
You have heard how the story of Gilgamesh was written down on clay tablets by the priests of Babylon. These priests could read the stars and foretell the future, and they invented the measure of time which we still use today. But they also had other wisdom. When Gilgamesh asked them if all men must die, they answered: "On an island far away lives a man who is your great-great-great-grandfather. His name is Ut-Naphistim and he was born in Atlantis before it sank under the sea. If you find him, you will also find the secret of life without end, life without death."

When he heard this Gilgamesh left his kingdom and the city of Erek, and set out alone on a journey to the island of his ancestor, Ut-Naphistim. Terrible were the adventures he met on this long, long journey. He came to a mountain which reached so high into the sky with valleys that plunged down so deeply that he could not see where it began. Then he saw an opening in the side of the mountain guarded by two strange creatures. The upper half of their bodies, their heads, arms and chests were like those of men, but from the waist down they were scorpions (a kind of poisonous insect). They were as tall as towers, and when Gilgamesh saw them even he, the fearless one, fainted.

But the two scorpion men did not harm him and, after he had recovered, they asked him why he had come. When Gilgamesh told them he was seeking the island of Ut-Naphistim, the scorpion men said: "The way lies through this mountain. But we must warn you not to go on with your journey. It is man's destiny to die!" But Gilgamesh answered: "I must find the secret of life without death." And the monsters allowed him to enter the cave, which was like a great tunnel through the mountain.

As Gilgamesh walked through the tunnel, it became darker and darker until he was in complete pitch black darkness. On and on he walked, without a glimmer of light for twenty four hours. He was near despair and thought he would never see the sun again, when it began to get lighter. He rushed on, tired as he was, and soon there was daylight. And when Gilgamesh came to the end of the tunnel, a garden such as no man had ever seen lay before him. The trees in the garden bore no ordinary fruit but shining jewels: red rubies, green emeralds and blue sapphires.

But Gilgamesh did not linger in that garden of wonders. He passed through quickly and soon came to the shore of a great sea. After a long search on the shore he found a ferryman and a boat. But the ferryman refused to take Gilgamesh across the water to the island where

Ut-Naphistim lived. It was only when Gilgamesh took an axe and began to smash the boat that the man quickly agreed to row him across the sea.

As they approached the island, Gilgamesh could see a tall man with a large white beard and snow-white hair falling on his shoulders standing on the shore. It was Ut-Naphistim. With him was his wife who was also white-haired. But they were both strong and full of vigour although they were many hundreds of years old.

Ut-Naphistim welcomed Gilgamesh and told him of ancient Atlantis and how the gods had destroyed it in a great flood. But Ea, the God of Wisdom, had warned Ut-Naphistim.

He had told him to build a ship to save his wife and his family. After the terrible rain, floods and earthquakes were over, Ea had given the secret of life without end to Ut-Naphistim and his wife. But the God of Wisdom had also said it should not be passed on to their children or to any other person.

Gilgamesh pleaded and pleaded with Ut-Naphistim and, in the end, the old man said: "I will give you the secret if you stay awake for six days and seven nights." Gilgamesh said: "I will," but he was so tired and exhausted from his long journey that he soon fell fast asleep. When he awoke, Gilgamesh again begged Ut-Naphistim to give him the secret of life without end. Ut-Naphistim's wife was so moved that she persuaded the old man.

But Ut-Naphistim said: "I will give you the secret, but it will do you no good because it is man's destiny on earth to die." Then he continued: "There is a deep lake on this island. Dive down to the bottom of that lake and you will see a green plant growing there in the water. It is the Plant of Life, and he who has that plant will remain healthy and strong and will never die. But I must warn you: on your way back to the city of Erek you must never sleep. If you fall asleep before you have reached Erek, the Plant of Life will be lost forever.

Gilgamesh went to the lake and dived down into the water. He found the green plant and brought it up with him. He thanked Ut-Naphistim and his wife. The ferryman rowed him back and even accompanied Gilgamesh to help him on his journey. They passed through the dark cave and did not see the scorpion men. And all the time Gilgamesh had not slept. At last they came near the city of Erek, and Gilgamesh sent the ferryman ahead so that the city would prepare a great welcome for their king.

It was a hot day and Gilgamesh sat down by a sparkling brook for a short rest. He was very thirsty, but as he bent down to drink he was suddenly overcome by sleep. And while Gilgamesh slept, a snake came along and carried away the Plant of Life. When Gilgamesh woke he cried bitter tears over his loss. He knew he would not find another plant. And he knew he would have to die as all men on earth have to die. But there was one thought which gave him comfort, hope and strength: that when he died he would be together again with his friend Eabani.

And that is the end of the strange story written in cuneiform letters on tablets by the wise priests of Babylon.

Myths of Egypt

The Gift of the Nile

If you compare the three ancient lands of India, Persia and Babylonia, you can see how human beings slowly learnt to feel more and more at home on earth. At first, in India, people did not care much for life on earth. They were really looking forward to the time when they would die and leave earth behind.

Later, in Persia, men became farmers and peasants. They began to like life on earth, but they still looked forward to going to the Kingdom of Light after death. Still later, in Babylon, people were much more at home on earth. They built cities, they watched the stars, they measured time. But the more they liked life on earth, the less they wanted to leave the earth; you heard how Gilgamesh tried very hard to find the secret of living on earth forever.

But now we come to another country where men began to like life on earth even more. This country is called Egypt and it is, first of all, a land without rain. Throughout the year there are perhaps ten days when there are clouds in the sky. There are maybe four or five days when a little rain falls; all the rest of the year the sky is clear and blue. It is scorching hot in summer and very warm in winter.

Now you know that where there is heat and practically no rain plants cannot grow, and when nothing grows human beings cannot live. However, Egypt is not an arid sun-scorched desert, without plants, animals or people. And this is because of the river Nile. The Nile rises far away, one thousand miles away from Egypt, in high snow-capped mountains. After a long journey, the waters of the

Nile flow through the country until they reach the sea. Yet the river itself would not be much help if it was not for something else.

For eleven months of the year, the waters of the Nile roll slowly through the hot dusty plains that stretch on either side of it. But each year at the end of August something extraordinary happens. The river becomes troubled and swift. As it begins to flow faster and faster, the water turns red and then green. The river rises until it is twenty four feet (or four times a man's height) higher than it was before. Then it overflows its banks and floods the country.

The whole valley through which the Nile flows becomes one vast lake. But the surrounding villages rise above the water like islands, for they have all been built on artificial or man-made mounds. But what happens to make the river Nile rise? In August, in the mountains far away where the Nile has its source, very heavy rain falls. A vast amount of mud and earth is swept down by the water, which turns the river red and green. After three or four weeks, the rain stops and the flood subsides. The river returns to its old bed and flows quietly on for the next eleven months. But it leaves behind all the mud and earth it brought from the mountains.

Into this thick layer of rich soil the people of Egypt sow their crops each year and the warm sun does the rest. Things grow very quickly and in four months time they can harvest. Every year a new layer of fresh soil comes down the river Nile, so they don't have to bother about manure or fertilisers. So although it is a land of very little rain, Egypt is also a country where many crops are grown. And you can see why it is called 'a gift of the Nile.' Without the river Nile, Egypt would remain a bare, empty desert.

Just as Babylonia was the Land of Two Rivers, so Egypt is the land of one river. And on the banks of that river, magnificent cities, palaces and temples were built. Even today, after five thousand years, people from all over the world come to look with awe and wonder at the great works of the ancient Egyptians. Later on you will hear something about these things: the pyramids, the treasures in the tombs of the kings, and the preserved bodies of the dead, or mummies, as they were called. But first you shall hear the story of how it all began, the story as it was told by the ancient Egyptians.

The Egyptians had many gods but the highest, the god they worshipped above all others, was the Sun God. And the God of the Sun, the spirit which guides the sun across the sky, was the great god Ra. The people of Egypt also said it was Ra who made the river Nile. He put his arm and hand down on the land and when he lifted it up, it left a deep imprint. That imprint is the bed of the river, and if you look at a map of Egypt you will see that the course of the Nile looks like a long arm. Where the river flows into the sea it opens out into several branches like fingers on a hand.

Now, Ra wanted the Egyptian people to be taught the right way of living, including how to use the soil which the Nile gave every year. So one day he called two other gods, the god Osiris and his wife, Isis, and told them they should live as human beings on earth to teach the ancient Egyptians all they needed to learn.

Isis and Osiris

Music Like a Magic Spell

At the beginning in ancient Egypt, the people still lived in small tribes that wandered hither and thither hunting wild animals. There were often disagreements between tribes which led to war and bloodshed. But you remember that Ra had asked the god Osiris and his wife, Isis, to take on human form and live on earth. And one day two travellers, a man and a woman, both tall and stately, arrived among these tribes people. They did something no one had seen or heard before: the man played on a hollow piece of bamboo with holes in it, and the woman sang.

For the first time in the world there was the sound of music on earth. It was very wonderful music for it was made by two divine beings, by Osiris and Isis, and these primitive people listened with awe and wonder. Osiris carried no weapons but nobody would have lifted a hand against the strangers, for the music was like a magic spell.

Then Osiris and Isis spoke to them. The people listened eagerly for the strangers seemed to know so much. They spoke with such wisdom that the tribes people felt they were no ordinary human beings. And, in time, one tribe after another asked Osiris and Isis to become their king and queen. So it happened that Osiris and Isis ruled all these tribes people who, not so long ago, had been at war with one another.

A new way of life began. The people built houses from mud bricks, but they built them on top of little hillocks or mounds, so the village would not be flooded when the Nile rose. Osiris showed them not only how to plant seeds of wheat and barley for their food, but also how to grow flax. And in turn, Isis taught people how flax could be spun and woven into linen to make clothing. As Egypt is a hot country people do not need warm clothing. So the men dressed in a white linen kilt or skirt and the women wore a long tight-fitting dress, also made of white linen.

But it was not only the rich fertile soil from the Nile that Osiris taught people to use. He also showed them how to dig canals from the river into their fields. When the flood had gone and the Nile flowed again in the old river-bed, water came through the canals to the fields. By using buckets people could water the plants, which would otherwise have died in the heat of the sun.

Yet it was not only in matters of food and clothing that the Egyptians learned from King Osiris. You remember that the river Nile spreads out in several branches, like the fingers on a hand, before it flows into the sea. The land between these fingers was swamp land, so it was no use for growing crops. But there were some plants that grew very well in this swampy ground. They were called reeds or papyrus.

These reeds were quite useless, until the wise King Osiris showed people what could be done if the stems were

Figure 1:

The word 'eat' in hieroglyphics. The eye stands for 'e', the apple for 'a' and the tree for the letter 't'.

cut and the outer skin stripped. Inside was a finer skin that was carefully removed in long white strips. These strips were put on a wooden board, one layer running across horizontally and the next running down vertically. Water was poured over them and then the layers were beaten and beaten with flat wooden beaters until there was a white, thin pulp. When the pulp dried, it was just like a sheet of coarse paper. And this paper, made of beaten papyrus skins, was the first paper in the world.

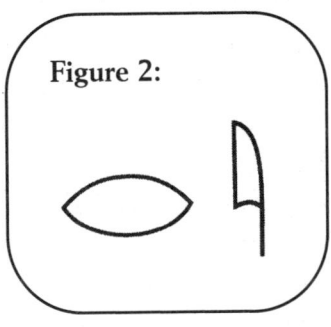

Figure 2:

After King Osiris had shown his people how to make paper, he taught them how to write on it. He made ink from soot mixed with a little glue, called gum arabic, so that it would stick to the paper. And he wrote with a pointed reed. But the writing Osiris showed the Egyptians was not like our writing, nor was it like the wedge-shaped cuneiform writing of Babylonia. King Osiris taught people a picture writing called hieroglyphics.

Picture writing (see Figure 1) was a slow way of communicating but this was how real writing on paper began, just think of how long it would take you to write a page in hieroglyphics. Yet that was how people wrote in ancient Egypt; writing in pictures and every picture stood for the first letter of the word.

For instance the word for mouth was *re*, and the word for feather was *at*, so when the Egyptians wanted to write the name of the god Ra they drew a picture of a mouth, and a picture of a feather (Figure 2). *Re* and *at* meant Ra, but just to be sure you understood it was the name of the God of the Sun, they also wrote the sign for the sun (Figure 3).

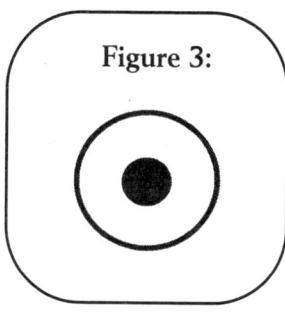

Figure 3:

Because this picture writing was taught by King Osiris, who was really a god, it was treated as something holy and the word hieroglyphics actually means 'holy writing.' In the early days of Egypt it was only used for very holy and very important things such as prayers, or stories of the laws of the gods, rather than the everyday things we use writing for. Osiris and Isis brought great blessings to the people of Egypt. There were just and fair laws. There was peace and the people were happy and content under the rulership of the wise king and queen. But there are always evil powers who fight goodness and happiness wherever they find it, and so it was after Osiris and Isis had ruled for many years.

A Coffin for the King

You have heard of the blessings which Osiris and Isis brought to the people of Egypt. The primitive lives of the tribes people changed after they heard the music the gods played. They learned to use the fertile soil of the Nile to grow food and to weave beautiful white linen cloth. They built villages on mounds and dug canals to water their crops. They also made paper and wrote on it with holy picture writing, or hieroglyphics.

Now it happened that Osiris had an evil brother called Set who was also a god. Set envied Osiris for his wisdom and hated him for his goodness. His only desire was to harm Osiris, so he took on human form to try and destroy the good work done by his brother. He became a king and ruled over African tribes.

But Set made his people savage and cruel, and several times the evil brother led his fierce warriors against Egypt. They burnt the crops and killed whole villages but each time the armies of Osiris came and drove the cruel invaders out.

Then Set knew that he could do very little by force and he thought of a way to overcome Osiris by cunning.

One day he sent a messenger to Osiris to say: "Are we not brothers? Let us live in peace and friendship from now on. Let us have a great banquet and eat and drink together to celebrate the end of all the fighting." Osiris, of course, believed his brother and invited him to the palace for a great feast to mark the end of the war. And so Set arrived, accompanied by seventy two of his black warriors, and Osiris received him with love.

Isis, the queen, did not trust Set and she said to Osiris: "Your brother is treacherous. If he speaks kind words there is sure to be some evil purpose behind it. Please, do not take part in this banquet." But Osiris answered: "He is my brother and he has learnt at last that peace is better than war. I am very happy that he has changed. Surely, it would be wrong for me not to celebrate this occasion with him."

But when evening came and the banquet began in the great hall of the palace, Queen Isis went to her room to rest. She would not join a party which included the evil Set. But sleep did not come, for her heart was heavy with anxiety and fear for her husband.

In the meantime the banquet had been served. Dish after dish of choice food arrived, and beautiful maidens filled the cups of courtiers and warriors with sparkling wines. Together they toasted Osiris and Set who sat next to each other. Towards the end of the feast, Set said: "The craftsmen of Egypt are famous for their skill. But I have brought something from foreign lands which no Egyptian craftsmen can equal."

He went to a corner of the hall where his men had put down something large that was covered with a cloth. He took the cloth off and everyone gasped. What they saw was a beautifully carved wooden chest inlaid with strange patterns in gold and gleaming jewels. The great box glittered in the candle light and was exquisite to behold.

When all the people in the hall had admired the chest, Set said: "As you all see, the chest is so large that a man can easily lie down in it. Now, to celebrate this feast of love and peace between my brother Osiris and myself, I will give this beautiful chest as a gift to the person who fits into it best." The whole company cheered when they heard that, and one man after another climbed in and lay down to see how well he fitted into the chest. But many of them were too short so their feet did not touch the end, and the men who were long enough were too thin.

All had tried, except Osiris. "Now it is your turn, dear brother," said Set with a crafty smile. Osiris rose from his seat and lay down in the chest. He fitted perfectly, as if the chest had been made to measure. But as soon as his brother was in the chest, Set gave a fierce shout of triumph and slammed the lid down. He slid home the bolts which fastened the lid, and some of his followers came running with hammers and nails to make sure Osiris could not escape.

Meanwhile, Set's remaining warriors brought out weapons they had hidden under their clothes and fell upon the courtiers of King Osiris. They were completely taken by surprise and in a few moments they had all been killed. Then Set cried: "Into the river with the chest." His men quickly lifted the box and carried it down to the Nile and threw it in. And at that moment a great flame of light came from the chest. It lasted only for a moment, then it was gone, and the box was carried away down the river by a swift current.

Queen Isis had fallen into a fitful sleep, haunted by terrible dreams. Shivering, she awoke but she could hear no sound from the banqueting hall. Then she heard voices outside, voices that came from the river. She hurried to the window, just in time to see a great chest being thrown into the Nile by Set and his men. When the queen saw the flames of light that shone for a moment, she knew that the divine spirit of Osiris had left his body. Isis realised that the chest was a coffin with the dead body of her husband, Osiris, inside.

She knew, too, that at any moment Set and his men would come for her. Quickly, Isis spoke the strange words of a spell. She was still saying the spell when Set's wild warriors came back from the river and stormed into the palace. But when they rushed into her room they saw no queen. All they found was a swallow which took wing and flew out through the open window and disappeared into the darkness.

That same night, Set's black warriors poured from all sides into Egypt. Without a king or queen to lead them, the Egyptians had no heart to resist and the treacherous, evil Set became master and king of Egypt.

And Isis, poor Isis, went in search of her husband's body.

The Search for Osiris

You remember how Set tricked his brother Osiris into lying down in a carved wooden chest which became a coffin for his dead body. The river Nile carried the box away and Queen Isis, who had escaped from Set and his warriors, went in search of her husband's body. For many weeks the coffin floated on the waves of the river Nile. But the body inside the coffin did not decay as other human bodies do; it remained always as it had been in the hour of Osiris's death.

Now, you see, for thousands of years, long after it all had happened, the people of Egypt remembered the great and good King Osiris. And every Egyptian wanted, when he died, to be buried in a coffin like that of King Osiris. He also wanted his body to remain unchanged by death, just as the body of Osiris did not change after death. But ordinary human bodies do change after death. They decay and, after a time, become dust. So the Egyptians invented a special way to treat dead bodies by preserving or embalming them.

It was quite a difficult, complicated treatment to preserve the body. There were specially trained people who knew how to embalm; that is they knew the spices myrrh and cassia would preserve the body. After embalming, the body was laid for seventy days in nitre or saltpetre. It was then wrapped up in hundreds of yards of linen bandages, and placed in a wooden coffin.

The coffin was shaped like a human form so that it fitted as closely to the body as possible, in the same way that Osiris fitted the carved chest. When a king died, the coffin was inlaid with gold and jewels, but even the coffins of poorer people were covered with paintings and hieroglyphics. And where the head of the corpse lay, the coffin was shaped like a face.

But the coffins of kings were not just buried, they were put into a great tomb or house of the dead. On the walls of these tombs, which were sometimes caves in a mountainside, paintings or sculptures showed what the dead person had done in life. These painted pictures of the dead man's life might show him fighting in battles, hunting lions, supervising work in the fields or feasting. Quite often a king's most precious treasures, such as jewels and golden vessels, were also buried in the tomb with him. And that is one reason why we know a great deal about life in ancient Egypt: it can all still be seen on the walls of the tombs.

But also the men who embalmed the bodies and turned them into mummies did their work so well that a number of examples can be seen today in many museums. Of course, they are not quite unchanged; the skin of the mummies has turned black, and you can see the bones under the skin. But even now, after five thousand years, you can still see what these people looked like.

Now, you heard Queen Isis had set out to find her husband's coffin. Long and weary was her search, for the swiftly flowing currents of the Nile had carried the coffin out to sea. At last, in a faraway country called Phoenicia, near the city of Byblos, the coffin was thrown ashore. It was a stormy night when this happened and waves as high as houses crashed on to the shore. One huge wave threw the coffin into the branches of a tree that stood near the seashore of Byblos. For a few days it rested in the branches of the tree but, being a heavy box, it then slipped down into the hollow trunk.

Days later, the king of the city of Byblos walked along the shore past the tree. He said to the men who were with him: "I need a new wooden pillar to hold up the roof of my palace. Yonder tree is just right for it, cut it down and take it to the palace." The men did so and no one noticed that there was something inside the thick hollow trunk. And so the trunk, with the coffin inside, became a pillar which helped hold up the roof of the palace of the king of Byblos in Phoenicia.

Soon after, Queen Isis arrived weary and exhausted in the city of Byblos. One night she dreamt she saw a wooden pillar and inside the pillar was the coffin containing the body of her husband, Osiris. The next morning she went past the king's palace and saw the same pillar she had seen in her dream. However, Isis did not quite know how she could get the tree trunk when it was being used to help support the roof of the palace.

But it happened at that time that the young son of the king of Byblos had fallen ill and none of the doctors could cure the child. Day by day he wasted away and his parents, the king and queen, were desperate. When Isis heard the people in the streets talk about the child's illness, she knew what she had to do. She went to the palace and came before the king and offered to cure his child.

The king of Byblos said: "If you can cure my son you can have all the gold in my treasury, even my golden crown or anything you like!" Then Isis walked to the room where the little boy was lying in his cot. His face was flushed with fever and his eyes were closed. When the goddess laid her cool hands on the child's head, his face turned a healthy colour and the boy opened his eyes and smiled at her. The next day he was up and running about with his playmates as if he had never been ill.

The king was overjoyed but he was very surprised when Isis asked for the wooden pillar as a reward, rather than gold or treasure. Then Queen Isis told the king of Byblos who she was and why she wanted that pillar. When he heard her story, the king gave immediate orders to take the pillar down and put another in its place. The coffin, which was still inside the pillar, was given to Isis. And the wooden pillar itself was taken to a temple where it was treated as something holy by the people of Byblos for hundreds of years.

The Birth of Horus
Before we go on with the story of Isis, let us think again about the mummies of Egypt. Do you remember the story about Cilgamesh? Because he was afraid of dying, Gilgamesh went on a long journey to find the secret of life without end. But the snake took the precious Plant of Life.

Now, the Egyptians did not think of life without end. They knew people had to die, but they thought they could at least keep the dead as life-like as possible. And that is really why they made mummies. They were so fond of their bodies that they did not want them to become dust. They wanted to preserve the body even after death, as long as possible.

Just think of this: the people of ancient India were not fond of their bodies at all. When a man died in India his body was burned on a pyre, so that it became ashes and dust very quickly. Then during the time of Persia and Babylonia, people became more and more fond of life on earth and of their bodies. But later still, during the time of ancient Egypt, people were so fond of their bodies that, after death, they were embalmed and made into mummies.

So you see how things change in the world as time passes. A queen of India, for instance, would not have worried so much about finding the dead body of her husband, but Isis, the queen of Egypt, went on a long search until she found the coffin in a wooden pillar at the palace of the king of Byblos in Phoenicia.

Now the king of Byblos gave Isis not only the coffin but also a sailing boat. She put the coffin in the boat, blessed the king and then set out across the sea. And so she returned to Egypt, where the evil Set was still king. His soldiers searched everywhere for Isis and she had to hide in swamp land, overgrown with papyrus reeds, where the Nile spreads out in branches like the fingers of a hand.

There, in the swamps of the Nile, Isis kept the coffin with the body of Osiris hidden, waiting for the time when it could be given a proper royal burial. And while she was in hiding, Queen Isis gave birth to a son, called Horus. She hoped with all her heart that the day would come when Horus would punish the evil Set and become the ruler of Egypt.

But Set and his men did not cease searching for her. And one night, the wisest of the gods of Egypt, whose name was Thoth, appeared to Isis in a dream. If you were to see the god Thoth in a dream you would not like him much. He had a human body but the head of a bird, a stork-like bird called an ibis which has a long curved beak.

However, the people of ancient Egypt thought that the animals were in many ways much wiser than human beings. And they said: "Birds can fly thousands of miles and find their way to far distant places and back without maps or compasses. And have you ever seen how beautifully a honey-comb is made? The bees make it without the help of rulers. So every animal has some wisdom which is more than human cleverness." And because this wisdom was given to the animals by the gods, the Egyptians worshipped many gods which had either animal or bird's heads.

So the god Thoth, with the ibis head, appeared to Isis in her dream and told her that early next morning Set and his followers would come to the swamp. When Isis woke up it was still dark. She took Horus and quickly left the swamp. But the precious coffin had to remain behind, for she could not carry it and her child.

Early the next day Set and his men came searching, and they soon found the coffin hidden in the papyrus. Set shouted with glee as the coffin was opened. Then the evil brother did something horrible: on his command the body of Osiris was taken out and cut up into fourteen pieces. All the pieces were then thrown into the Nile so that the crocodiles in the river would eat them. Yet even the ferocious crocodiles would not touch the holy body of Osiris. Instead the pieces were carried along by the river and, after a time, one bit after another was washed up on to the banks of the Nile.

Once again poor Isis set out to find her husband's body. Wherever she went the people of Egypt, who hated the evil Set, helped her and her child Horus. Wherever she found each piece of the body of Osiris, it was buried and the people built a temple to mark the place. Eventually thirteen temples were dotted along the banks of the Nile and they remained holy places of worship for many hundreds of years. But the fourteenth piece of Osiris was never found.

And although Set and his followers continued to search for Isis, the people of Egypt always warned her in time. They kept Isis hidden and helped her so that she was never captured. And in time, Horus grew up and became a strong man and a brave warrior. All over Egypt men secretly made weapons; swords and spears, battle-axes and arrows, to join the fight against Set as soon as Horus gave the command.

One night the spirit of Osiris came to Horus in a dream. Osiris appeared in royal robes and said: "My son, since I have left the earth, I have become the great judge of all human souls. Every man who dies comes before me and must give an account of his life on earth. The good deeds and evil deeds are written down by the wise Thoth. And on a great set of scales the heart of each man is weighed. Cruel, selfish, untruthful hearts weigh little, while kind, unselfish, truthful hearts have great weight.

The spirit of Osiris continued: "And when all the deeds are written down and the heart has been weighed, I, Osiris, pronounce judgment. The good men and women are welcomed into my kingdom, but the wicked ones are sent to the realm of darkness where they have monsters and demons for companions. And I, Osiris, the Judge of the Dead, call you now to take up arms and free Egypt from the evil tyrant Set."

Weighing the Souls of the Dead
The god Osiris had become the judge of dead souls. Now the ancient Egyptians wrote down on their papyrus rolls what happened to a soul after it left the embalmed or mummified body. In great detail they described the journey the soul makes after death. At first such a soul had to pass through a dark valley where monsters and demons lay in wait. But these creatures were powerless against a good soul who could pass through without fear. But because the soul of a wicked person was full of fear, the monsters would seem fierce. Such a soul would take a long time to travel through the dark valley.

Ahead lay a great river where a ferryman and a boat waited. As the ferryman rowed the soul across the water, he kept his face turned away and never uttered a word. In silence, the soul was ferried across the river to the land of the dead where stood the mighty Hall of Judgment. At the gate a god with the body of a man and the head of a jackal (a fox-like animal) met the soul and accompanied it into the great hall where Osiris sat on a throne.

Before Osiris, stood an enormous set of scales and beside the scales was the ibis-headed god, Thoth, with papyrus and reed to write down the soul's deeds. There was also a monster with a crocodile's head ready to take away the souls of the wicked, while around the hall sat many other gods who would speak for and against the soul that was being judged. And before that assembly of mighty gods who looked so grave, the soul of a man could not speak anything but the truth. No one could lie or pretend in the great Hall of Judgment.

If, in life, a soul had been good, it would say the words learnt on earth, the words which are written on papyrus rolls in the graves and tombs of Egypt: "I have done no wrong against any man. I have never given my servants too much work. I have never cheated when selling goods or given false measure. My scales have always been true. I have not caused pain or suffering to any man. I have not told lies or untruth. I have not taken that which is not mine. I have not committed murder."

Then the jackal-headed god weighed the whole life of the soul on the scales. But how can one weigh a whole life? It was a very strange kind of weighing for on one side of the scales was nothing but a single feather, and a feather is the sign of truth. On the other scale there was a little vessel shaped like a heart. Every good deed, or true word spoken, made the heart-shaped vessel heavier and heavier, while every untruth or evil deed made it lighter. So, if the soul had belonged to a wicked person, the scale with the feather on it went down.

Thoth, the ibis-headed god, then called out the result of the weighing. If it was the soul of a good person, Osiris would say: "He has gained victory. Let him dwell with the gods in the fields of *Aalu* (the heavens)." But if the soul was wicked, the crocodile-headed monster dragged it away. And every Egyptian knew they would come before Osiris in this way and be judged in the great Hall of Judgment after death.

Now you have heard how Osiris appeared to his son Horus in a dream and told him to fight against the treacherous Set. Horus obeyed; all over Egypt brave men were waiting to fight Set for they all had suffered under the rule of the wicked king. Set's soldiers stole what they liked without punishment, they threw anyone who dared to speak against them to the crocodiles in the Nile and, on days when they were bored, they burnt houses and crops just for fun. So when Horus gave the command and called on people to take up arms and fight the oppressor, the men of Egypt obeyed with joy. And before that great army marched into battle, Isis came and blessed the warriors and promised that those who died fighting for Horus would be received with love by his father, Osiris, the Judge of the Dead.

The greatest city in Egypt at that time was Thebes and it was there that the armies of Horus and Set clashed. Set and his men knew they could expect no mercy from Horus so they fought fiercely, and for a long time neither side could win. Then Horus came upon Set on the battlefield and, when these two met, all the others stopped fighting and watched.

Set was older and more experienced, and his cunning blows struck and wounded Horus again and again. But with the strength of youth, Horus rallied again and again. That evening as the sun set, Horus, with a mighty effort, drove his sword into the black heart of Set. The evil king fell to the ground and a black cloud rose into the air, just as a flame of light had appeared when Osiris had died. That black cloud was the spirit of Set, who was also a divine being but an evil one, and now he had left the earth.

When Set fell, his men fled in all directions, but few escaped from the swords of the Egyptians. Horus and Isis entered the city of Thebes in triumph, and Horus became the king of Egypt.

The Great Pyramids
In time, Queen Isis died and returned to the gods. And Horus, too, after many years of peaceful reign, left the earth and became the god of the rising and setting sun. You remember Ra was also the god of the sun but he ruled the sun when it stood at its highest at midday. Now you know when the sun rises and sets, it is over the horizon or the most distant line you can see. And the word horizon comes from Horus; the line of Horus is the horizon we talk about today.

But the ancient Egyptians did not count the hours of the day as we do. They said the first hour of the day was the hour after sunrise, rather than the way we think of it with the new day beginning after midnight. For the Egyptians, the new day began from the hour of sunrise or Horus. And of course the word hour also comes from Horus. So without knowing it, we still remember Horus, the son of Osiris, in the words horizon and hour that we use today.

Now because the first kings of Egypt, Osiris and Horus and even Set, had been gods who for a time lived in human form, all the later kings, or pharaohs as they were called, were regarded as gods in human shape. Every command of a king was obeyed as if a god had spoken. Enormous statues of kings were put up in public places, so that people would look up in awe and feel their king watched over them just like a god.

The people of ancient Egypt were also the first in the world to build things from stone. But they did not use it to make their own houses or even the palaces of kings. The great palaces of the god-like kings or pharaohs were built from wood, while ordinary people lived in mud brick houses. They never lasted long and had to be rebuilt again and again. What they did make of stone were the buildings for the gods. These temples to the gods were made to last and they were made so well that many of them, filled with inscriptions, are still standing today.

The greatest of these works in stone, made by the Egyptians, are the pyramids. You may have heard that the pyramids are the tombs of kings, but this is not quite true. Inside the pyramids there are rooms or chambers. And in those rooms the old priests taught their most precious knowledge and wisdom to the younger priests.

In our time, all the knowledge we have is passed on to as many young people as possible. But in ancient Egypt knowledge was regarded as something holy. The old priests picked only the very best of young students, those who were good and clever, and those students were taught in special places like the pyramids.

So the pyramids were a kind of temple and university at the same time. What was taught was knowledge that was kept secret and not passed on to other people. What it was exactly we don't know, for such secrets were not written down. But it seems likely the students learned ways to see the gods and to hear the gods, so that their will could be done on earth.

There are quite a number of smaller pyramids in Egypt. But the three greatest pyramids are at Giza, not far away from the capital, called Cairo. The largest of the three is the famous pyramid built by King Kufu (or Cheops). It is four hundred and eighty feet high, and it sits in the desert like a huge rock. But it is a rock made by man, a rock made of mighty slabs of stone. Each stone weighs about two-and-a-half tons and there are two million of these stones.

But the wonder of all this is that when this great pyramid was built, the Egyptians had no machines. They had no iron at all; the only metal they used was copper which is not very hard. Nor do we know how they cut these enormous stones in their quarries. The quarries are miles away across the river Nile, so how did they transport the stones over that distance? And how did they raise such huge stones higher and higher as the pyramids grew?

We can only guess the answers. There must have been hundreds of thousands of workers. Perhaps the two million stones were each put on rollers made of tree trunks, for instance, and slowly pulled by hundreds of men to the building site. And to raise the stones maybe the Egyptians made ramps of earth, a kind of slope which was not very steep. Then they pulled the stones up these earth slopes.

Another wonderful thing about the great pyramids is the way the stones are so carefully cut. They are so perfectly smooth that, unlike bricks, they are not held together by mortar or cement. Each stone fits its neighbour above, below, and to either side so exactly that you could not put a razor blade between them.

The great pyramid of Kufu is one of the wonders of the world. Yet it was built without iron, without machines, and without cement. You remember that the Babylonians, the people of the Land of Two Rivers, were the first to measure time. But the first people to measure stones so precisely were the Egyptians. They were the first people who built with stones and who knew how to measure absolutely correctly.

Near the site of the pyramids there is a great natural rock, sticking out from the desert. This great rock was carved in the likeness of a man's head with a lion's body, and is known as the sphinx. It sits there like a guardian. Perhaps it keeps guard over the long-held secrets taught by the priests in the chambers of the pyramids of ancient Egypt.

Appendix

The following material was extracted from the main text in order to maintain the narrative flow. In the context of a classroom situation, the author's intention was to actively and imaginatively illustrate the time span involved in the passage of 10,000 years.

The people who told these stories you will hear lived very far back in time, so let us try to work out how far back we have to go. You are now ten years old. When were your parents ten years old? About 25 years ago. And your grandparents were ten years old about 50 years ago. So your great-grandparents were ten years old 75 years ago, and their parents, your great-great-grandparents, were ten a hundred years ago.

Now if one of you stands for all the ten-year-olds alive today, another for the parents, another for the grandparents (when they were ten), another for the great-grandparents, and yet another for the great-great-grandparents then that takes us back 100 years. Now if another four children stand, for four more generations, that's 200 years. Another four makes 300 years and another four comes to 400 years and 16 children.

So you can see we would need five classes of 16 children to make 2000 years which was the time when Christ lived on earth. But we have to go still further back to come to the time of which I want to tell you. Let's take another five classes of about 16 children. That will take us to 2000 years before Christ, and another five classes makes 4000 years before Christ. So to count back 10,000 years in time we would need 400 children, or two schools like ours.

Further reading

Ancient Myths – Their meaning and connection with evolution by R. Steiner, Steiner Book Centre, Vancouver

Chapters from Ancient History by Dorothy Harrar, AWSNA, USA.

Christianity as Mystical Fact by R. Steiner, SteinerBooks, USA.

Egyptian Myths and Mysteries by R. Steiner, SteinerBooks.

From Sphinx to Christ by E. Schure, SteinerBooks.

Myths from Mesopotamia translated by S. Dalley, Oxford University Press, England.

Occult History by R. Steiner, Rudolf Steiner Press, England.

Myths of the World by P. Colum, Floris Books, Edinburgh.

Rudolf Steiner's Curriculm for Waldorf Schools by Karl Stockmeyer, Steiner Waldorf Schools Fellowship, England.

Tales of Ancient Egypt edited by R. Lancelyn Green, Puffin Books, England.

The Epic of Gilgamesh translated and edited by Andrew George, Penguin Books, England.

The *Mysteries of the East and of Christianity* by R. Steiner, SteinerBooks.

True and False Paths in Spiritual Investigation by R. Steiner, Rudolf Steiner Press.

Universe, Earth and Man by R. Steiner, Rudolf Steiner Press.

The Great Initiates — A study of the secret history of religion by E. Schure, SteinerBooks.

On publication of this book the following titles were out of print, but are recommended if available:

World History and the Mysteries in the Light of Anthroposophy by R. Steiner, Rudolf Steiner Press.

Ancient Egypt by C. A. Burland, Hulton Educational Publications

The Bhagavad Gita and the West by R. Steiner. SteinerBooks.

Other books by Charles Kovacs

The following titles are published by Floris Books

The Age of Discovery
The Age of Revolution
Ancient Greece
Ancient Rome
Botany
Muscles and Bones
Parsifal, And the Search for the Grail
The Spiritual Backghround to Christian Festivals
The Human Being and the Animal World.